T0007454

Misconceptions about the Tuskegee Airmen

Misconceptions about the Tuskegee Airmen

Refuting Myths about America's First Black Military Pilots

Daniel Haulman

NEW SOUTH BOOKS
an imprint of
The University of Georgia Press
Athens

NSB

Published by NewSouth Books,
an imprint of the University of Georgia Press
Athens, Georgia 30602
https://ugapress.org/imprints/newsouth-books/

© 2023 by Daniel L. Haulman
All rights reserved
Designed by Mary McKeon
Set in Adobe Garamond Pro
Printed and bound by Sheridan

The paper in this book meets the guidelines for
permanence and durability of the Committee on
Production Guidelines for Book Longevity of the
Council on Library Resources.

Most NewSouth/University of Georgia Press titles are
available from popular e-book vendors.

Printed in the United States of America
27 26 25 24 23 P 5 4 3 2 1

Library of Congress Control Number: 2022948467
ISBN: 9781588384546 (paperback)
ISBN: 9781588384799 (e-book)

Contents

Misconceptions about the Tuskegee Airmen

Introduction

The members of the 332d Fighter Group and the 99th, 100th, 301st, and 302d Fighter Squadrons during World War II are remembered in part because they were the only African American pilots who served in combat with the U.S. armed forces during World War II. Because they trained at Tuskegee Army Air Field before and during the war, they are sometimes called the Tuskegee Airmen.

For decades after the 1945 conclusion of World War II, few people had ever heard of the Tuskegee Airmen or even knew that black fighter pilots flew in combat in World War II. After publication of the first book about them, in 1955, and especially after the release of two motion pictures about them, one in the 1990s and another in the second decade of the twenty-first century, they have become legendary. In fact, the Tuskegee Airmen's 332d Fighter Group has become better known than any of the other fighter groups in the Fifteenth Air Force in World War II.

In the more than seventy years since World War II, several stories have surfaced about the Tuskegee Airmen, many of them true, but many of them false. There are so many false stories about the Tuskegee Airmen that their true story is sometimes in danger of being overshadowed by myths and distortions. If one does not know which of the stories is false and which is true, one might wonder what to believe. This book distinguishes fact from fiction so that the reader can see the true history.

This book debunks fifty-five misconceptions about the Tuskegee Airmen. It is based firmly on the evidence, most of which consists of primary-source documentation at the Air Force Historical Research Agency, where the author worked as a historian for more than thirty years. That documentation includes periodic histories of the 332d Fighter Group and the 477th Bombardment Group, and the eight squadrons that were assigned to them (histories written during World War II by Tuskegee Airmen themselves), the 332d Fighter Group's daily narrative mission reports (also written by Tuskegee Airmen immediately after the missions); orders issued by the Twelfth and Fifteenth Air Forces; Fifteenth Air Force mission folders; missing air crew reports; and histories of Tuskegee Army Airfield.

The goal of this book is certainly not to demean or defame the Tuskegee Airmen or to take away from them the glory they deserve; it is, in fact, quite the opposite. Many if not most of the misconceptions originated not among the Tuskegee Airmen themselves but from other sources, including people who repeated hearsay as if it were fact and inflated what they heard. Readers aware of what is false will develop a greater appreciation for the true story of the Tuskegee Airmen and what they accomplished for themselves, for their country, and for civil rights. The record of the Tuskegee Airmen is outstanding without any embellishments, and they deserve an indelible place of honor among America's military heroes of World War II.

1

The misconception of inferiority

The idea that the Tuskegee Airmen were inferior to their white colleagues is rooted in the racist myth that black men were inferior to white men and lacked the ability to perform certain tasks, such as flying a fighter effectively in combat.

The airplane was invented in 1903, and the military acquired its first airplanes and pilots in 1909, but black men were not allowed to be pilots in the American military until the 1940s. During World War I, there were no black pilots in the American military. In October 1925, the U.S. Army War College issued a memorandum titled "The Use of Negro Manpower in War," which reflected the racial prejudice of the white army leaders of the time. It claimed that black Americans were inferior to white Americans, encouraged continued segregation within the army, and recommended that African Americans be allowed to do certain menial tasks but not tasks that would require more intelligence.[1]

In 1941, President Franklin D. Roosevelt directed the War Department to begin training black pilots, which the Army Air Corps reluctantly began to do—but only on a segregated basis. The first class of black pilots in the U.S. military graduated in March 1942, and they were assigned to the 99th Fighter Squadron, the first black flying unit in American history. A little more than a year later, the 99th Fighter Squadron finally was allowed to deploy overseas for combat, but only while attached to white fighter groups.

One of those white fighter groups was the 33d. Its commander, Col. William Momyer, did not want a black squadron attached to his group and became convinced that it should be taken out of combat because of poor performance. In September 1943, Momyer sent his recommendation to Maj. Gen. Edwin J. House, commander of the XII Air Support Command, who forwarded it to Maj. Gen. John K. Cannon, deputy commander of the Northwest African Tactical Air Force.[2]

The so-called House memorandum went all the way up the chain of command to the headquarters of the Army Air Forces. In response, the War Department conducted an official study to compare the performance of the 99th Fighter Squadron with that of other P-40 units in the Twelfth Air Force. The subsequent report, released on March 30, 1944, concluded that the 99th

Fighter Squadron had performed as well as the white P-40 squadrons with which it flew in the Mediterranean Theater of Operations. The 99th Fighter Squadron was allowed to stay in combat, although it was attached to another white fighter group.[3]

In the meantime, the 332d Fighter Group, the first black flying group, and its three squadrons, the 100th, 301st, and 302d Fighter Squadrons, deployed to Italy for combat duty. In the summer of 1944, the 332d Fighter Group began a new mission of escorting heavy bombers for the Fifteenth Air Force, and the 99th Fighter Squadron was assigned to it. For the bomber escort mission, the Tuskegee Airmen began flying red-tailed P-51 Mustang airplanes, the best fighters in the Army Air Forces. Their range and speed allowed them to protect bombers against enemy fighters.

During its combat with the Fifteenth Air Force, the 332d Fighter Group was one of seven fighter escort groups, four that flew P-51s and three that flew P-38s. During the period from June 1944 to the end of April 1945, the 332d Fighter Group shot down more enemy airplanes than two of the other groups, both of which flew P-38s. In other words, the Tuskegee Airmen shot down more enemy airplanes than two of the white fighter escort groups in the same period, but the fewest enemy airplanes compared with the other three P-51 units.[4]

It is possible that the Tuskegee Airmen shot down fewer enemy aircraft than the other P-51 fighter groups—and had no aces with five aerial victory credits—because they were staying closer to the bombers they were escorting. The total number of Fifteenth Air Force bombers shot down by enemy aircraft between June 1944 and May 1945, when the 332d Fighter Group was assigned to the Fifteenth Air Force, was 303. The total number of 332d Fighter Group–escorted bombers shot down by enemy aircraft was twenty-seven. Subtracting 27 bombers from the 303 total shot down by enemy aircraft leaves 276 bombers shot down by enemy aircraft while under the escort of one or more of the other six fighter groups in the Fifteenth Air Force. Dividing 276 by six, one finds that 46 is the average number of bombers shot down by enemy aircraft when those bombers were under the escort of one of the other fighter groups. The Tuskegee Airmen lost only twenty-seven, significantly fewer bombers than the average number lost by the other fighter groups in the Fifteenth Air Force. In other words, the Tuskegee Airmen lost significantly fewer bombers to enemy airplanes than average of the other fighter groups in the Fifteenth Air Force.[5] In terms of numbers of enemy aircraft shot down, the Tuskegee Airmen's record was worse than that of the other P-51 groups in the same period, but in terms of the number of bombers that returned safely under their protection, the Tuskegee Airmen's record was better.

Years after World War II, some of the Tuskegee Airmen remembered false claims that standards had been lowered for them, as if they would not have become U.S. military pilots if they had had to meet the same standards as the white pilots. Col. Noel Parrish, commander of the basic and advanced flying school at Tuskegee Army Air Field, insisted on maintaining standards just as high as those for white pilots and even suffered criticism for allowing so many of the black cadets to be eliminated or "washed out" for failing to meet those standards. Only about half of black cadets who entered the flight-training program at Tuskegee graduated from advanced flight training. Those African Americans who did graduate as Army Air Forces pilots had met the same exacting standards as the white pilots at other training bases and were equal to them in skill.

TABLE 1 · Fighter Groups of the Fifteenth Air Force in World War II

Organization	Total Aerial Victories, June 1944–April 1945
1st Fighter Group	72
14th Fighter Group	85
31st Fighter Group	278
52d Fighter Group	224.5
82d Fighter Group	106
325th Fighter Group	252
332d Fighter Group	94

Sources: USAF Historical Study No. 85, "USAF Credits for the Destruction of Enemy Aircraft, World War II" (Washington, D.C.: Office of Air Force History, 1978); Maurer Maurer, Air Force Combat Units of World War II (Washington, D.C.: Office of Air Force History, 1983).

TABLE 2 · Fifteenth Air Force Heavy Bombers Lost, June 1944–May 1945 (When 332d Fighter Group Assigned to Fifteenth Air Force)

Month	Year	Number of Heavy Bombers Lost to Enemy Aircraft
June	1944	85
July	1944	94
August	1944	91
September	1944	7
October	1944	0
November	1944	1
December	1944	18
January	1945	0
February	1945	0
March	1945	7
April	1945	0
May	1945	0
Total	June 1944–April 1945	303

Source: Army Air Forces Statistical Digest for World War II, 1946 (Washington, D.C.: Statistical Control Division, Office of Air Comptroller, June 1947), 256 (table 160)

2

The misconception of "never lost a bomber"

Another misconception that developed during the last months of the war is the story that no bomber under escort by the Tuskegee Airmen was ever shot down by enemy aircraft. A version of this misconception appears in Alan Gropman's book *The Air Force Integrates*: "Their record on escort duty remained unparalleled. They never lost an American bomber to enemy aircraft."[1] This misconception originated, in the press, even before the end of World War II. A version of the statement first appeared in a March 10, 1945, issue of *Liberty Magazine*, in an article by Roi Ottley, who claimed that the black pilots had not lost a bomber they escorted to enemy aircraft in more than one hundred missions. The 332d Fighter Group had by then flown more than two hundred missions. Two weeks after Ottley's article, on March 24, 1945, another article appeared in the *Chicago Defender* claiming that in more than two hundred missions, the group had not lost a bomber they escorted to enemy aircraft. In reality, bombers under Tuskegee Airmen escort were shot down on seven different days: June 9, 1944; June 13, 1944; July 12, 1944; July 18, 1944; July 20, 1944; August 24, 1944; and March 24, 1945.[2] Moreover, the Tuskegee Airmen flew 312 missions for the Fifteenth Air Force between early June 1944 and late April 1945, and only 179 of those missions escorted bombers.

Alan Gropman interviewed General Benjamin O. Davis Jr. years after World War II, and specifically asked him if the "never lost a bomber" statement was true. General Davis replied that he questioned the statement, but that it had been repeated so many times people were coming to believe it.[3] Davis himself must have known the statement was not true, because his own citation for the Distinguished Flying Cross, contained in Fifteenth Air Force General Order 2972 dated August 31, 1944, noted that on June 9, 1944, "Colonel Davis so skillfully disposed his squadrons that in spite of the large number of enemy fighters, the bomber formation suffered only a few losses."[4]

To determine whether or not bombers under the escort of the Tuskegee Airmen were ever shot down by enemy aircraft during World War II, I practiced the following method.

First, I determined which bombardment wing the Tuskegee Airmen were escorting on a given day and when and where that escort took place. I found this information in the daily narrative mission reports of the 332d Fighter

Group, which are filed with the group's monthly histories from World War II. The call number for these documents at the Air Force Historical Research Agency is GP-332-HI followed by the month and year.

Next, I determined which bombardment groups were in the bombardment wing that the Tuskegee Airmen were escorting on the day in question. I found this information in the daily mission folders of the Fifteenth Air Force. The Fifteenth Air Force daily mission folders also contain narrative mission reports for all the groups that took part in missions on any given day, including reports of both the fighter and bombardment groups, as well as the wings to which they belonged. The call number for these documents at the Air Force Historical Research Agency is 670.332 followed by the date. The bombardment group daily mission reports show which days bombers of the group were shot down by enemy aircraft.

Next, I checked the index of the Missing Air Crew Reports to see if the groups that the Tuskegee Airmen were escorting that day lost any aircraft. If any aircraft of those groups were lost that day, I recorded the missing air crew report numbers. This index of Missing Air Crew Reports is located in the archives branch of the Air Force Historical Research Agency. The Missing Air Crew Reports usually confirmed the bomber loss information contained in the bombardment group daily narrative mission reports.

Finally, I looked at the individual Missing Air Crew Reports of the Tuskegee Airmen–escorted groups that lost airplanes on that day to see when the airplanes were lost, where the airplanes were lost, and whether the airplanes were lost because of enemy aircraft fire, enemy antiaircraft fire, or some other cause. The Missing Air Crew Reports note that information for each aircraft lost, with the aircraft type and serial number, and usually also contain witness statements that describe the loss. For lost bombers, the witnesses were usually the crew members of other bombers in the same formation, or members of the crews of the lost bombers themselves, after they returned. The Missing Air Crew Reports are filed on microfiche in the archives branch of the Air Force Historical Research Agency.

Using this procedure, I determined conclusively that on at least seven days, bombers under the escort of the Tuskegee Airmen's 332d Fighter Group were shot down by enemy aircraft. Those days include June 9, 1944; June 13, 1944; July 12, 1944; July 18, 1944; July 20, 1944; August 24, 1944; and March 24, 1945.[5]

TABLE 3 • Bombers Shot Down by Enemy Aircraft While Flying in Groups the 332d Fighter Group Was Assigned to Escort

Date	Time	Location	Type	Serial Number	WG	GP	Macr
June 9, 1944	0905	46 40 N, 12 40 E	B-24	42-78219	304	459	6317
June 9, 1944	0907	46 00 N, 12 40 E	B-24	42-52318	304	459	6179
June 13, 1944	0900	Porogruardo, Italy	B-24	42-94741	49	484	6097
July 12, 1944	1050	20 miles SE of Mirabeau, France	B-24	42-52723	49	461	6894
July 12, 1944	1051	10 miles E of Mirabeau, France	B-24	42-78202	49	461	6895
July 12, 1944	1105	43 43 N, 05 23 E	B-24	42-78291	49	461	7034
July 18, 1944	1045–1100	near Memmingen	B-17	42-107179	5	483	6856
July 18, 1944	1045–1100	near Memmingen	B-17	42-107008	5	483	6953
July 18, 1944	1045–1100	near Memmingen	B-17	42-102862	5	483	6954
July 18, 1944	1045–1100	near Memmingen	B-17	44-6174	5	483	6975
July 18, 1944	1045–1100	near Memmingen	B-17	42-97671	5	483	6976
July 18, 1944	1045–1100	near Memmingen	B-17	42-102382	5	483	6977
July 18, 1944	1045–1100	near Memmingen	B-17	42-107170	5	483	6978
July 18, 1944	1045 1100	near Memmingen	B-17	42-102923	5	483	6979
July 18, 1944	1045–1100	near Memmingen	B-17	42-102927	5	483	6980
July 18, 1944	1045–1100	near Memmingen	B-17	42-97584	5	483	6981
July 18, 1944	1045–1100	near Memmingen	B-17	42-46267	5	483	7097
July 18, 1944	1045–1100	near Memmingen	B-17	42-102422	5	483	7098
July 18, 1944	1045–1100	near Memmingen	B-17	44-6177	5	483	7099
July 18, 1944	1045–1100	near Memmingen	B-17	42-107172	5	483	7153
July 18, 1944	1104	47 54 N, 10 40 E	B-17	42-102943	5	301	7310
July 20, 1944	1000	45 38 N, 12 28 E	B-24	44-40886	55	485	6914
July 20, 1944	0954	45 38 N, 12 28 E	B-24	42-78361	55	485	6919
Aug. 24, 1944	1245-1247	49 28 N, 15 25 E	B-17	42-31645	5	97	7971
Mar. 24, 1945	1200	52 05 N, 13 10 E	B-17	44-6283	5	463	13278
Mar. 24, 1945	1208	51 00 N, 13 10 E	B-17	44-6761	5	463	13274
Mar. 24, 1945	1227	Berlin target area	B-17	44-8159	5	463	13375

Primary Sources: Daily mission reports of the 332d Fighter Group AFHRA, call number GP-332-HI); daily mission reports of the bombardment groups the 332d Fighter Group was assigned to escort per day, from the daily mission folders of the Fifteenth Air Force AFHRA, call number 670.332); microfiche of Missing Air Crew Reports (MACRs) at the AFHRA, indexed by date and group.

3

The misconception of the deprived ace

Another popular misconception that circulated after World War II is that white officers were determined to prevent any black man in the Army Air Forces from becoming an ace, and therefore reduced the aerial victory credit total of Lee Archer from five to less than five to accomplish their aim. A version of this misconception appears in the Oliver North compilation *War Stories III,* which quotes Lee Archer as saying "I figure somebody up the line just wasn't ready for a black guy to be an ace." In the same source, Archer claimed that one of his five victories was reduced to a half, and no one knew who got the other half.[1] Another version of the story is contained in an interview of Lee Archer by Dr. Lisa Bratton conducted on March, 13, 2001, in New York, New York, in which Archer claimed that he shot down five enemy airplanes, without specifying the dates, and that one of his victories was cut in half and given to another pilot named Freddie Hutchins, leaving him with 4.5. He also claimed, in the same interview, that the American Fighter Aces Association honored him, implying that the association had named him an ace at last.[2]

In reality, according to the World War II records of the 332d Fighter Group and its squadrons (which were very carefully kept by members of the group), Lee Archer claimed a total of four aerial victories during World War II, and received credit for every claim.[3] Moreover, there is no evidence that Lt. Freddie Hutchins earned any half credit, with the other half credit going to Archer. In fact, Hutchins earned a full credit for shooting down an enemy aircraft on July 26, 1944. The mission report for that day, which lists all the claims from the mission, does not list Archer.[4] The order that awarded the credit to Hutchins on July 26 was issued on August 6, 1944, and it was the same order that awarded a credit to Archer for July 18, 1944.[5]

The misconception that Lee Archer was an ace was perpetuated in part because of an excerpt in the book *The Tuskegee Airmen* by Charles E. Francis. In that book, Francis mentions an aerial victory for Archer on July 20, 1944, but the history of the 332d Fighter Group for July 1944, the mission report of the 332d Fighter Group for July 20, 1944, and the aerial victory credit orders issued by the Fifteenth Air Force in 1944 do not support Francis's claim. The documents show that Lee Archer did not claim to have shot down an enemy aircraft that day and did not receive credit for such a claim, either.[6]

World War II documents, including monthly histories of the 332d Fighter Group and Twelfth and Fifteenth Air Force general orders awarding aerial victory credits, show that Lee Archer claimed and was awarded a total of four aerial victory credits during World War II, one on July 18, 1944, and three on October 12, 1944. There is no evidence among these documents that Lee Archer ever claimed to have destroyed any more than four enemy aircraft in the air during the war, and he was never awarded any more than four. A fifth was never taken away or downgraded to half. Moreover, there is no evidence, among the documents, that there was any effort to prevent any members of the 332d Fighter Group from becoming aces. If someone had reduced one of Archer's July credits to a half, or taken it away entirely, that person would have had no way of knowing that Archer would get credit for three more aircraft months later, in October, and approach ace status. When claims were made, they were recorded and evaluated by a victory credit board that decided, using witness statements and gun camera film, whether to award credits, which were confirmed by general orders of the Fifteenth Air Force. There is no evidence that the black claims were treated any differently than the white claims. If there had been such discrimination in the evaluation of claims, Col. Benjamin O. Davis, Jr. the leader of the group, would have most likely complained, and there is no evidence of any such complaint. To think that someone or some group was totaling the number of aerial victory credits of each of the members of the various squadrons of the 332d Fighter Group and intervening to deny credit to anyone who might become an ace is not consistent with the aerial victory credit procedures of the day.

During World War II, the only African American pilots in the Army Air Forces who flew in combat served in the 99th, 100th, 301st, and 302d Fighter Squadrons and the 332d Fighter Group. None of these pilots earned more than four aerial victory credits. None of them became an ace, with at least five aerial victory credits. Were the Tuskegee Airmen who earned four aerial victory credits sent home in order to prevent any black pilots from becoming aces?

This is very doubtful. First Lt. Lee Archer was deployed back to the United States the month after he scored his fourth aerial victory credit, and the same month he received his fourth aerial victory credit. Capt. Edward Toppins was deployed back to the United States the second month after he scored his fourth aerial victory credit, the month after he received credit for it. However, Capt. Joseph Elsberry earned his fourth aerial victory credit in July 1944 and received credit for it early in August 1944. He did not redeploy to the United States until December 1944. If there was a policy of sending Tuskegee Airmen with four aerial victory credits home in order to prevent a black man from

TABLE 4 · Chronological Table of 332d Fighter Group Aerial Victory Credits

Date	Name	Unit	Downed	GO #
July 2, 1943	1 Lt. Charles B. Hall	99 FS	1 FW-190	32 XII ASC Sep. 7, 1943
Jan. 27, 1944	2 Lt. Clarence W. Allen	99 FS	0.5 FW-190	66 XII AF May 24, 1944
	1 Lt. Willie Ashley Jr.	99 FS	1 FW-190	122 XII AF Aug. 7, 1944
	2 Lt. Charles P. Bailey	99 FS	1 FW-190	66 XII AF May 24, 1944
	1 Lt. Howard Baugh	99 FS	1 FW-190 0.5 FW-190	122 XII AF Aug 7, 1944 66 XII AF May 24, 1944
	Cpt. Lemuel R. Custis	99 FS	1 FW-190	122 XII AF Aug. 7, 1944
	1 Lt. Robert W. Deiz	99 FS	1 FW-190	66 XII AF May 24, 1944
	2 Lt. Wilson V. Eagleson	99 FS	1 FW-190	66 XII AF May 24, 1944
	1 Lt. Leon C. Roberts	99 FS	1 FW-190	122 XII AF Aug. 7, 1944
	2 Lt. Lewis C. Smith	99 FS	1 FW-190	66 XII AF May 24, 1944
	1 Lt. Edward L. Topplns	99 FS	1 FW-190	81 XII AF June 22, 1944
Jan. 28, 1944	1 Lt. Robert W. Deiz	99 FS	1 FW-190	122 XII AF Aug. 7, 1944
	Cpt. Charles B. Hall	99 FS	1 FW-190 1 ME-109	64 XII AF May 22, 1944
Feb. 5, 1944	1 Lt. Elwood T. Driver	99 FS	1 FW-190	66 XII AF May 24, 1944
Feb. 7, 1944	2 Lt. Wilson V. Eagleson	99 FS	1 FW-190	122 XII AF Aug. 7, 1944
	2 Lt. Leonard M. Jackson	99 FS	1 FW-190	66 XII AF May 24, 1944
	1 Lt. Clinton B. Mills	99 FS	1 FW-190	66 XII AF May 24, 1944
June 9, 1944	1 Lt. Charles M. Bussy	302 FS	1 ME-109	1473 XV AF June 30, 1944
	2 Lt. Frederick D. Funderburg	301 FS	2 ME-109s	1473 XV AF June 30, 1944
	1 Lt. Melvin T. Jackson	302 FS	1 ME-109	1473 XV AF June 30, 1944
	1 Lt. Wendell O. Pruitt	302 FS	1 ME-109	1473 XV AF June 30, 1944
July 12, 1944	1 Lt. Harold E. Sawyer	301 FS	1 FW-190	2032 XV AF July 23, 1944
	1 Lt. Joseph D. Elsberry	301 FS	3 FW-190	2466 XV AF Aug. 10, 1944
July 16, 1944	1 Lt. Alfonza W. Davis	332 FG	1 MA-205	2030 XV AF July 23, 1944
	2 Lt. William W. Green Jr.	302 FS	1 MA-202	2029 XV AF July 23, 1944
July 17, 1944	1 Lt. Luther H. Smith Jr.	302 FS	1 ME-109	2350 XV AF Aug. 6, 1944
	2 Lt. Robert H. Smith	302 FS	1 ME-109	2350 XV AF Aug. 6, 1944
	1 Lt. Laurence D. Wilkins	302 FS	1 ME-109	2350 XV AF Aug. 6, 1944
July 18, 1944	2 Lt. Lee A. Archer	302 FS	1 ME-109	2350 XV AF Aug. 6, 1944
	1 Lt. Charles P. Bailey	99 FS	1 FW-190	2484 XV AF Aug. 11, 1944
	1 Lt. Weldon K. Groves	302 FS	1 ME-109	2350 XV AF Aug. 6, 1944

Continued

Date	Name	Unit	Downed	GO #
July 18, 1944	1 Lt. Jack D. Holsclaw	100 FS	2 ME-109s	2202 XV AF July 31, 1944
	2 Lt. Clarence D. Lester	100 FS	3 ME-109s	2202 XV AF July 31, 1944
	2 Lt. Walter J. A. Palmer	100 FS	1 ME-109	2202 XV AF July 31, 1944
	2 Lt. Roger Romine	302 FS	1 ME-109	2350 XV AF Aug. 6, 1944
	Cpt. Edward L. Toppins	99 FS	1 FW-190	2484 XV AF Aug. 11, 1944*
	2 Lt. Hugh S. Warner	302 FS	1 ME-109	2350 XV AF Aug. 6, 1944
July 20, 1944	Cpt. Joseph D. Elsberry	301 FS	1 ME-109	2284 XV AF Aug. 3, 1944
	1 Lt. Langdon E. Johnson	100 FS	1 ME-109	2202 XV AF July 31, 1944
	Cpt. Armour G. McDaniel	301 FS	1 ME-109	2284 XV AF Aug. 3, 1944
	Cpt. Edward L. Toppins	99 FS	1 ME-109	2484 XV AF Aug. 11, 1944
July 25, 1944	1st Lt. Harold E. Sawyer	301 FS	1 ME-109	2284 XV AF Aug. 3, 1944
July 26, 1944	1 Lt. Freddie E. Hutchins	302 FS	1 ME-109	2350 XV AF Aug. 6, 1944
	1 Lt. Leonard M. Jackson	99 FS	1 ME-109	2484 XV AF Aug. 11, 1944
	2 Lt. Roger Romine	302 FS	1 ME-109	2350 XV AF Aug. 6, 1944
	Cpt. Edward L. Toppins	99 FS	1 ME-109	2484 XV AF Aug. 11, 1944
July 27, 1944	1 Lt. Edward C. Gleed	301 FS	2 FW-190s	2284 XV AF Aug. 3, 1944
	2 Lt. Alfred M. Gorham	301 FS	2 FW-190s	2284 XV AF Aug. 3, 1944
	Cpt. Claude B. Govan	301 FS	1 ME-109	2284 XV AF Aug. 3, 1944
	2 Lt. Richard W. Hall	100 FS	1 ME-109	2485 XV AF Aug. 11, 1944
	1 Lt. Leonard M. Jackson	99 FS	1 ME-109	2484 XV AF Aug. 11, 1944
	1 Lt. Felix J. Kirkpatrick	302 FS	1 ME-109	2350 XV AF Aug. 6, 1944
July 30, 1944	2 Lt. Carl E. Johnson	100 FS	1 RE-2001	2485 XV AF Aug. 11, 1944
Aug. 14, 1944	2 Lt. George M. Rhodes Jr.	100 FS	1 FW-190	2831 XV AF Aug. 25, 1944
Aug. 23, 1944	FO William L. Hill	302 FS	1 ME-109	3538 XV AF Sep. 21, 1944
Aug. 24, 1944	1 Lt. John F. Briggs	100 FS	1 ME-109	3153 XV AF Sep. 6, 1944
	1 Lt. Charles E. McGee	302 FS	1 FW-190	3174 XV AF Sep. 7, 1944
	1 Lt. William H. Thomas	302 FS	1 FW-190	449 XV AF Jan. 31, 1945
Oct. 12, 1944	1 Lt. Lee A. Archer	302 FS	3 ME-109s	4287 XV AF Nov. 1, 1944
	Cpt. Milton R. Brooks	302 FS	1 ME-109	4287 XV AF Nov. 1, 1944
	1 Lt. William W. Green Jr.	302 FS	1 HE-111	4287 XV AF Nov. 1, 1944
	Cpt. Wendell O. Pruitt	302 FS	1 HE-111 1 ME-109	4287 XV AF Nov. 1, 1944
	1 Lt. Roger Romine	302 FS	1 ME-109	4287 XV AF Nov. 1, 1944
	1 Lt. Luther H. Smith Jr.	302 FS	1 HE-111	4604 XV AF Nov. 21, 1944

Date	Name	Unit	Downed	GO #
Nov. 16, 1944	Cpt. Luke J. Weathers	302 FS	2 ME-109s	4990 XV AF Dec. 13, 1944
Mar. 16, 1945	1 Lt. William S. Price III	301 FS	1 ME-109	1734 XV AF Mar., 24, 1945
Mar. 24, 1945	2 Lt. Charles V. Brantley	100 FS	1 ME-262	2293 XV AF Apr. 12, 1945
	1 Lt. Roscoe C. Brown	100 FS	1 ME-262	2293 XV AF Apr. 12, 1945
	1 Lt. Earl R. Lane	100 FS	1 ME-262	2293 XV AF Apr. 12, 1945
Mar. 31, 1945	2 Lt. Raul W. Bell	100 FS	1 FW-190	2293 XV AF Apr. 12, 1945
	2 Lt. Thomas P. Brasswell	99 FS	1 FW-190	2292 XV AF Apr. 12, 1945
	1 Lt. Roscoe C. Brown	100 FS	1 FW-190	2293 XV AF Apr. 12, 1945
	Maj. William A. Campbell	99 FS	1 ME-109	2292 XV AF Apr. 12, 1945
	2 Lt. John W. Davis	99 FS	1 ME-109	2292 XV AF Apr. 12, 1945
	2 Lt. James L. Hall	99 FS	1 ME-109	2292 XV AF Apr. 12, 1945
Mar. 31, 1945	1 Lt. Earl R. Lane	100 FS	1 ME-109	2293 XV AF Apr. 12, 1945
	FO John H. Lyle	100 FS	1 ME-109	2293 XV AF Apr. 12, 1945
	1 Lt. Daniel L. Rich	99 FS	1 ME-109	2292 XV AF Apr. 12, 1945
	2 Lt. Hugh J. White	99 FS	1 ME-109	2292 XV AF Apr 45
	1 Lt. Robert W. Williams	100 FS	2 FW-190s	2293 XV AF Apr. 12, 1945
	2 Lt. Bertram W. Wilson Jr.	100 FS	1 FW-190	2293 XV AF Apr. 12, 1945
Apr. 1, 1945	2 Lt. Carl E. Carey	301 FS	2 FW-190s	2294 XV AF Apr. 12, 1945
	2 Lt. John E. Edwards	301 FS	2 ME-109s	2294 XV AF Apr. 12, 1945
	FO James H. Fischer	301 FS	1 FW-190	2294 XV AF Apr. 12, 1945
	2 Lt. Walter P. Manning	301 FS	1 FW-190	2294 XV AF Apr. 12, 1945
	2 Lt. Harold M. Morris	301 FS	1 FW 190	2294 XV AF Apr. 12, 1945
	1 Lt. Harry T. Stewart	301 FS	3 FW-190s	2294 XV AF Apr. 12, 1945
	1 Lt. Charles L. White	301 FS	2 ME-109s	2294 XV AF Apr. 12, 1945
Apr. 15, 1945	1 Lt. Jimmy Lanham	301 FS	1 ME-109	3484 XV AF May 29, 1945
Apr. 26, 1945	2 Lt. Thomas W. Jefferson	301 FS	2 ME-109s	3362 XV AF May 23, 1945
	1 Lt. Jimmy Lanham	301 FS	1 ME-109	3362 XV AF May 23, 1945
	2 Lt. Richard A. Simons	100 FS	1 ME-109	2990 XV AF May 4, 1945

* Order says credit was July 16, 1944, but history says July 18, 1944.

becoming an ace, the case of Capt. Joseph Elsberry contradicts it, because he was not sent home until four months after his fourth aerial victory credit was awarded, and five months after he scored it. It is more likely that the pilots who deployed back to the United States did so after having completed the number of missions they needed to finish their respective tours of duty.

Finally, the American Fighter Aces Association did honor Lee Archer one year but did not in fact name him an ace. At the same meeting, Charlton Heston was honored, but he was not named an ace either. Frank Olynyk, a historian for the American Fighter Aces Association, confirmed that the association never recognized Lee Archer as having shot down five enemy aircraft, and Olynyk's account agrees with that of the Air Force Historical Research Agency: Lee Archer earned a total of four aerial victory credits.[7]

A related myth about the Tuskegee Airmen is the notion that there were many black pilots, not just Lee Archer, who shot down at least five enemy airplanes, but because of racism, they were not given credit and were denied ace status. The histories of the 99th, 100th, 301st, and 302d Fighter Squadrons, and of the 332d Fighter Group, written by Tuskegee Airmen themselves during the war, refute the myth. Those histories contain all the claims of black pilots for having shot down enemy airplanes, and they are consistent with the credits that were awarded by orders of the Twelfth or the Fifteenth Air Force. The Tuskegee Airmen shot down a total of 112 enemy airplanes, but none of the Tuskegee Airmen were aces. Four of the Tuskegee Airmen each shot down three enemy airplanes in one day, and three of the Tuskegee Airmen each shot down a total of four enemy airplanes, but there were no Tuskegee Airmen aces.[8]

The myth that Lee Archer was a black ace persists in other publications, such as the book *Mustang Aces of the Ninth and Fifteenth Air Forces and the RAF* by Jerry Scutts and Chris Davy. This book claims that Archer destroyed one enemy aircraft on July 18, one on July 19, and three on October 12, 1944, for a total of five. The histories of the 332d Fighter Group for July and October 1944, and their attached daily narrative mission reports, do not support the claim. They confirm Archer's July 18 victory, and his three on October 12, which makes a total of four. I looked again at the July 1944 history of the group and the narrative mission reports, and the only aerial victory Archer

TABLE 5 • Table of Tuskegee Airmen with Four Aerial Victories

Name and Rank at Time of Fourth Aerial Victory Credit	Fighter Group	Fighter Squadron	Date of Fourth Aerial Victory	Date of Award of Fourth aerial Victory Credit	Month of Redeployment to the United States
1 Lt. Lee Archer	332	302	Oct. 12, 1944	Nov. 1, 1944	November 1944
Cpt. Joseph Elsberry	332	301	July 20, 1944	Aug. 3, 1944	December 1944
Cpt. Edward Toppins	332	99	July 26, 1944	Aug. 11, 1944	September 1944

Sources: Fifteenth Air Force general orders awarding aerial victory credits; monthly histories of the 332d Fighter Group for August, September, October, November, and December 1944, AFHRA

claimed in July was on July 18, and he received a credit for that. The 302d Fighter Squadron War Diary for the month, in the same set of documents, notes that Lt. Archer shot down one enemy airplane in July 1944, not two. Together with his three in October, Archer's total is four, not five. He is not, and never was, an ace, however much we might want to discover a black ace in World War II.[9]

4

The misconception of being first to shoot down German jets

In a March 30, 2007, American Forces Press Service article regarding the awarding of the Congressional Gold Medal to the Tuskegee Airmen, there is the statement that Tuskegee Airman Roscoe Brown was "the first U.S. pilot to down a German Messerschmitt jet."[1] That was another popular claim which has proven to be false. Lee Archer, one of the most famous Tuskegee Airmen, repeated the claim in a 2001 interview. He claimed that "guys like Roscoe Brown and three other people shot down the first jets in our history, in combat."[2] Three Tuskegee Airmen, 1st Lt. Roscoe Brown, 1st Lt. Earl R. Lane, and 2d Lt. Charles V. Brantley, each shot down a German Me-262 jet on March 24, 1945, during the longest Fifteenth Air Force mission, which went all the way to Berlin.[3] However, American pilots shot down no less than sixty Me-262 aircraft before March 24, 1945. Most of these American pilots served in the Eighth Air Force.[4]

The Tuskegee Airmen were also not the first Fifteenth Air Force pilots to shoot down German jets, as is sometimes alleged.[5] Two such pilots, 1st Lt. Eugene P. McGlauflin and 2d Lt. Roy L. Scales, both of the Fifteenth Air Force's 31st Fighter Group and 308th Fighter Squadron, shared a victory over an Me-262 German jet on December 22, 1944, and Capt. William J. Dillard, also of the Fifteenth Air Force's 31st Fighter Group and 308th Fighter Squadron, shot down an Me-262 German jet on March 22, 1945. Moreover, on the day three Tuskegee Airmen shot down three German jets over Berlin on March 24, 1945, five other American pilots of the Fifteenth Air Force, on the same mission, with the 31st Fighter Group, also shot down German Me-262 jets. They included Col. William A. Daniel, 1st Lt. Forrest M. Keene, 1st Lt. Raymond D. Leonard, Capt. Kenneth T. Smith, and 2d Lt. William M. Wilder.[6]

TABLE 6 · USAAF Aerial Victories over German Me-262 Jets

Date	Name	Credit	FTR GP	FTR SQ	Theater
Aug. 28, 1944	2 Lt. Manford O. Croy Jr.	.50	78	82 FS	ETO
Aug. 28, 1944	Maj. Joseph Myers	.50	78	82 FS	ETO
Oct. 7, 1944	Maj. Richard E. Conner	1.00	78	82 FS	ETO
Oct. 7, 1944	1 Lt. Urban L. Drew	2.00	361	375 FS	ETO
Oct. 15, 1944	2 Lt. Huie H. Lamb Jr.	1.00	78	82 FS	ETO
Nov. 1, 1944	1 Lt. Walter R. Groce	.50	56	63 FS	ETO
Nov. 1, 1944	2 Lt. William T. Gerbe Jr.	.50	352	486 FS	ETO
Nov. 6, 1944	Cpt. Charles E. Yeager	1.00	357	363 FS	ETO
Nov. 6, 1944	1 Lt. William J. Quinn	1.00	361	374 FS	ETO
Nov. 8, 1944	1 Lt. James W. Kenney	1.00	357	362 FS	ETO
Nov. 8, 1944	2 Lt. Anthony Maurice	1.00	361	375 FS	ETO
Nov. 8, 1944	1 Lt. Ernest C. Fiebelkorn Jr.	.50	20	77 FS	ETO
Nov. 8, 1944	1 Lt. Edward R. Haydon	.50	357	364 FS	ETO
Nov. 8, 1944	1 Lt. Richard W. Stevens	1.00	364	384 FS	ETO
Nov. 18, 1944	2 Lt. John M. Creamer	.50	4	335 FS	ETO
Nov. 18, 1944	Cpt. John C. Fitch	.50	4	335 FS	ETO
Dec. 9, 1944	2 Lt. Harry L. Edwards	1.00	352	486 FS	ETO
Dec. 22, 1944	1 Lt. Eugene P. McGlauflin	.50	31	308 FS	MTO
Dec. 22, 1944	2 Lt. Roy L. Scales	.50	31	308 FS	MTO
Jan. 13, 1945	1 Lt. Walter J. Konantz	1.00	55	338 FS	ETO
Jan. 14, 1945	1 Lt. Billy J. Murray	1.00	353	351 FS	ETO
Jan. 14, 1945	1 Lt. James W. Rohrs	.50	353	351 FS	ETO
Jan. 14, 1945	1 Lt. George J. Rosen	.50	353	351 FS	ETO
Jan. 15, 1945	1 Lt. Robert P. Winks	1.00	357	364 FS	ETO
Jan. 20, 1945	1 Lt. Dale E. Karger	1.00	357	364 FS	ETO
Jan. 20, 1945	2 Lt. Roland R. Wright	1.00	357	364 FS	ETO
Feb. 9, 1945	1 Lt. Johnnie L. Carter	1.00	357	363 FS	ETO
Feb. 9, 1945	Cpt. Donald H. Bochkay	1.00	357	363 FS	ETO
Feb. 9, 1945	1 Lt. Stephen C. Ananian	1.00	339	505 FS	ETO
Feb. 15, 1945	2 Lt. Dudley M. Amoss	1.00	55	38 FS	ETO
Feb. 21, 1945	1 Lt. Harold E. Whitmore	1.00	356	361 FS	ETO
Feb. 22, 1945	Cpt. Gordon B. Compton	1.00	353	351 FS	ETO
Feb. 22, 1945	2 Lt. Charles D. Price	1.00	352	486 FS	ETO
Feb. 22, 1945	Maj. Wayne K. Blickenstaff	1.00	353	350 FS	ETO

Continued

Date	Name	Credit	FTR GP	FTR SQ	Theater
Feb. 22, 1945	1 Lt. Oliven T. Cowan	1.00	388		ETO
Feb. 22, 1945	1 Lt. David B. Fox	1.00	366	391 FS	ETO
Feb. 25, 1945	Cpt. Donald M. Cummings	2.00	55	38 FS	ETO
Feb. 25, 1945	2 Lt. John F. O'Neil	1.00	55	38 FS	ETO
Feb. 25, 1945	Cpt. Donald E. Penn	1.00	55	38 FS	ETO
Feb. 25, 1945	1 Lt. Milliard O. Anderson	1.00	55	38 FS	ETO
Feb. 25, 1945	2 Lt. Donald T. Menegay	1.00	55	38 FS	ETO
Feb. 25, 1945	1 Lt. Billy Clemmons	1.00	55	38 FS	ETO
Feb. 25, 1945	1 Lt. Carl G. Payne	1.00	4	334 FS	ETO
Mar. 1, 1945	1 Lt. Wendell W. Beaty	1.00	355	358 FS	ETO
Mar. 1, 1945	1 Lt. John K. Wilkins Jr.	1.00	2 AD		ETO
Feb. 3, 1945	1 Lt. Theodore W. Sedvert	1.00	354	353 FS	ETO
Mar. 14, 1945	1 Lt. Charles R. Rodebaugh	1.00	2 AD	2 SF	ETO
Mar. 19, 1945	Maj. Niven K. Cranfill	1.00	359	368 FS	ETO
Mar. 19, 1945	Cpt. Robert S. Fifield	1.00	357	363 FS	ETO
Mar. 19, 1945	Maj. Robert W. Foy	1.00	357	363 FS	ETO
Mar. 19, 1945	Cpt. Charles H. Spencer	1.00	355	354 FS	ETO
Mar. 20, 1945	1 Lt. Robert E. Irion	1.00	339	505 FS	ETO
Mar. 20, 1945	1 Lt. Vernon N. Barto	1.00	339	504 FS	ETO
Mar. 21, 1945	Cpt. Edwin H. Miller	1.00	78	83 FS	ETO
Mar. 21, 1945	1 Lt. Richard D. Anderson	1.00	361	375 FS	ETO
Mar. 21, 1945	2 Lt. Harry M. Chapman	1.00	361	376 FS	ETO
Mar. 21, 1945	1 Lt. John A. Kirk III	1.00	78	83 FS	ETO
Mar. 21, 1945	1 Lt. Robert H. Anderson	1.00	78	82 FS	ETO
Mar. 21, 1945	2 Lt. Walter E. Bourque	1.00	78	82 FS	ETO
Mar. 21, 1945	Cpt. Winfield H. Brown	.50	78	82 FS	ETO
Mar. 21, 1945	1 Lt. Allen A. Rosenblum	.50	78	82 FS	ETO
Mar. 22, 1945	Cpt. William J. Dillard	1.00	31	308 FS	MTO
Mar. 22, 1945	2 Lt. John W. Cunnick III	1.00	55	38 FS	ETO
Mar. 22, 1945	1 Lt. Eugene L. Peel	.50	78	82 FS	ETO
Mar. 22, 1945	2 Lt. Milton B. Stutzman	.50	78	82 FS	ETO
Mar. 22, 1945	Cpt. Harold T. Barnaby	1.00	78	83 FS	ETO
Mar. 24, 1945	2 Lt. Charles V. Brantley	1.00	332	100 FS	MTO
Mar. 24, 1945	1 Lt. Roscoe C. Brown	1.00	332	100 FS	MTO

Date	Name	Credit	FTR GP	FTR SQ	Theater
Mar. 24, 1945	1 Lt. Earl R. Lane	1.00	332	100 FS	MTO
Mar. 24, 1945	Col. William A. Daniel	1.00	31	308 FS	MTO
Mar. 24, 1945	1 Lt. Forrest M. Keene Jr.	1.00	31	308 FS	MTO
Mar. 24, 1945	1 Lt. Raymond D. Leonard	1.00	31	308 FS	MTO
Mar. 24, 1945	Cpt. Kenneth T. Smith	1.00	31	308 FS	MTO
Mar. 24, 1945	2 Lt. William M. Wilder	1.00	31	308 FS	MTO
Mar. 25, 1945	1 Lt. Eugene H. Wendt	1.00	479	434 FS	ETO
Mar. 25, 1945	Maj. George E. Bostick	1.00	56	63 FS	ETO
Mar. 25, 1945	2 Lt. Edwin M. Crosthwait Jr.	1.00	56	63 FS	ETO
Mar. 25, 1945	Cpt. Raymond H. Littge	1.00	352	487 FS	ETO
Mar. 30, 1945	1 Lt. Patrick L. Moore	1.00	55	343 FS	ETO
Mar. 30, 1945	1 Lt. Carroll W. Bennett	1.00	339	504 FS	ETO
Mar. 30, 1945	Cpt. Robert F. Sargent	1.00	339	504 FS	ETO
Mar. 30, 1945	Lt. Col. John D. Landers	.50	78	38 FS	ETO
Mar. 30, 1945	2 Lt. Thomas V. Thain Jr.	.50	78	84 FS	ETO
Mar. 30, 1945	1 Lt. Kenneth J. Scott Jr.	1.00	361	376 FS	ETO
Mar. 30, 1945	1 Lt. James C. Hurley	1.00	352	328 FS	ETO
Mar. 30, 1945	2 Lt. John B. Guy	1.00	364	383 FS	ETO
Mar. 31, 1945	1 Lt. Marvin H. Castleberry	1.00	2 AD		ETO
Mar. 31, 1945	1 Lt. Harrison B. Tordoff	1.00	354	353 FS	ETO
Mar. 31, 1945	1 Lt. Wayne L. Coleman	1.00	78	82 FS	ETO
Mar. 31, 1945	Cpt. William T. Bales Jr.	1.00	371	406 FS	ETO
Apr. 4, 1945	1 Lt. Robert C. Coker	.50	339	504 FS	ETO
Apr. 4, 1945	Cpt. Kirke B. Everson Jr.	.50	339	504 FS	ETO
Apr. 4, 1945	Cpt. Nile C. Greer	1.00	339	504 FS	ETO
Apr. 4, 1945	2 Lt. Robert C. Havighurst	1.00	339	504 FS	ETO
Apr. 4, 1945	Lt. Col. George F. Ceuleers	1.00	364	383 FS	ETO
Apr. 4, 1945	1 Lt. Michael J. Kennedy	.50	4	334 FS	ETO
Apr. 4, 1945	1 Lt. Harold H. Frederick	.50	4	336 FS	ETO
Apr. 4, 1945	1 Lt. Raymond A. Dyer	1.00	4	334 FS	ETO
Apr. 4, 1945	Cpt. Harry R. Corey	1.00	339	505 FS	ETO
Apr. 4, 1945	1 Lt. John W. Haun	1.00	324	316 FS	ETO
Apr. 4, 1945	1 Lt. Andrew N. Kandis	1.00	324	316 FS	ETO
Apr. 5, 1945	Cpt. John C. Fahringer	1.00	56	63 FS	ETO

Continued

Date	Name	Credit	FTR GP	FTR SQ	Theater
Apr. 7, 1945	1 Lt. Hilton O. Thompson	1.00	479	434 FS	ETO
Apr. 7, 1945	Cpt. Verne E. Hooker	1.00	479	435 FS	ETO
Apr. 8, 1945	1 Lt. John J. Usiatynski	1.00	358	367 FS	ETO
Apr. 9, 1945	2 Lt. James T. Sloan	1.00	361	374 FS	ETO
Apr. 9, 1945	Maj. Edward B. Giller	1.00	55	343 FS	ETO
Apr. 10, 1945	Cpt. Gordon B. Compton	1.00	353	351 FS	ETO
Apr. 10, 1945	1 Lt. Harold Tenenbaum	1.00	359	369 FS	ETO
Apr. 10, 1945	2 Lt. Walter J. Sharbo	1.00	56	62 FS	ETO
Apr. 10, 1945	Cpt. John K. Hollins	1.00	20	79 FS	ETO
Apr. 10, 1945	Cpt. John K. Brown	1.00	20	55 FS	ETO
Apr. 10, 1945	1 Lt. Willmer W. Collins	1.00	4	336 FS	ETO
Apr. 10, 1945	2 Lt. John W. Cudd Jr.	.50	20	77 FS	ETO
Apr. 10, 1945	FO Jerome Rosenblum	.50	20	77 FS	ETO
Apr. 10, 1945	1 Lt. Keith R. McGinnis	1.00	55	38 FS	ETO
Apr. 10, 1945	2 Lt. Walter T. Drozd	1.00	20	77 FS	ETO
Apr. 10, 1945	2 Lt. Albert B. North	1.00	20	77 FS	ETO
Apr. 10, 1945	1 Lt. Robert J. Guggemus	1.00	359	369 FS	ETO
Apr. 10, 1945	1 Lt. Charles C. Pattillo	1.00	352	487 FS	ETO
Apr. 10, 1945	Lt. Col. Earl D. Duncan	.50	352	328 FS	ETO
Apr. 10, 1945	Maj. Richard G. McAuliffe	.50	352	328 FS	ETO
Apr. 10, 1945	1 Lt. Kenneth A. Lashbrook	1.00	55	338 FS	ETO
Apr. 10, 1945	Cpt. Robert W. Abernathy	1.00	353	350 FS	ETO
Apr. 10, 1945	1 Lt. Jack W. Clark	.50	353	350 FS	ETO
Apr. 10, 1945	2 Lt. Bruce D. McMahan	.50	353	350 FS	ETO
Apr. 10, 1945	1 Lt. Wayne C. Gatlin	1.00	356	360 FS	ETO
Apr. 10, 1945	1 Lt. Joseph W. Prichard	.50	352	487 FS	ETO
Apr. 10, 1945	2 Lt. Carlo A. Ricci	.50	352	487 FS	ETO
Apr. 10, 1945	Cpt. Douglas J. Pick	.50	364	384 FS	ETO
Apr. 10, 1945	1 Lt. Harry C. Schwartz	.50	364	384 FS	ETO
Apr. 16, 1945	1 Lt. Vernon O. Fein	1.00	368	397 FS	ETO
Apr. 16, 1945	1 Lt. Henry A. Yandel	1.00	368	397 FS	ETO
Apr. 16, 1945	Maj. Eugene E. Ryan	1.00	55	338 FS	ETO
Apr. 17, 1945	1 Lt. James Zweizig	1.00	371	404 FS	ETO
Apr. 17, 1945	Cpt. Jack A. Warner	1.00	354	356 FS	ETO

Date	Name	Credit	FTR GP	FTR SQ	Theater
Apr. 17, 1945	Cpt. Roy W. Orndarff	1.00	364	383 FS	ETO
Apr. 17, 1945	Cpt. Walter L. Goff	1.00	364	383 FS	ETO
Apr. 17, 1945	FO James A. Steiger	1.00	357	364 FS	ETO
Apr. 17, 1945	1 Lt. John C. Campbell Jr.	1.00	339	503 FS	ETO
Apr. 18, 1945	Maj. Ralph F. Johnson	1.00	325	319 FS	MTO
Apr. 18, 1945	Cpt. Charles E. Weaver	1.00	357	362 FS	ETO
Apr. 18, 1945	Maj. Donald H. Bochkay	1.00	357	363 FS	ETO
Apr. 19, 1945	Lt. Col. Jack W. Hayes Jr.	1.00	357	363 FS	ETO
Apr. 19, 1945	Cpt. Robert S. Fifield	1.00	357	363 FS	ETO
Apr. 19, 1945	1 Lt. Paul N. Bowles	1.00	357	363 FS	ETO
Apr. 19, 1945	1 Lt. Carroll W. Ofsthun	1.00	357	363 FS	ETO
Apr. 19, 1945	Cpt. Ivan L. McGuire	.50	357	364 FS	ETO
Apr. 19, 1945	1 Lt. Gilmon L. Weber	.50	357	364 FS	ETO
Apr. 19, 1945	1 Lt. Robert DeLoach	1.00	55	338 FS	ETO
Apr. 19, 1945	2 Lt. James P. McMullen	1.00	357	364 FS	ETO
Apr. 24, 1945	Cpt. Jerry G. Mast	.50	365	388 FS	ETO
Apr. 24, 1945	2 Lt. William H. Myers	.50	365	388 FS	ETO
Apr. 25, 1945	1 Lt. Richard D. Stevenson	.50	370	402 FS	ETO
Apr. 25, 1945	1 Lt. Robert W. Hoyle	.50	370	402 FS	ETO
Apr. 26, 1945	Cpt. Robert W. Clark	1.00	50	10 FS	ETO
Apr. 26, 1945	Cpt. Herbert A. Philo	1.00	27	522 FS	ETO

Sources: USAAF (European Theater) Credits for the Destruction of Enemy Aircraft in Air-to-Air Combat, World War 2, Victory List No. 5, Frank J. Olynyk, May 1987; USAAF (Mediterranean Theater) Credits for the Destruction of Enemy Aircraft in Air-to-Air Combat, World War 2, Victory List No. 6, Frank J. Olynyk, June 1987; USAF Historical Study No. 85, USAF Credits for the Destruction of Enemy Aircraft, World War II, Albert F. Simpson Historical Research Center, 1978; Combat Squadrons of the Air Force, World War II, edited by Maurer Maurer, 1969; Air Force Combat Units of World War II, edited by Maurer Maurer, 1983. Compiled by: Patsy Robertson, historian, Organizational Histories Branch, usafhra

5

The misconception that the Tuskegee Airmen sank a German destroyer

In the movie Red Tails by George Lucas, a P-51 fighter pilot is depicted as strafing a German destroyer until it explodes, and group members are later shown watching gun camera film of the attack and the explosion, suggesting that a Tuskegee Airman in a red-tailed Mustang sank a destroyer by himself. The 332d Fighter Group narrative mission report for June 25, 1944, notes that eight of the group's pilots flying P-47 aircraft strafed a German destroyer, on June 25, 1944, and two of them went around for another pass to do more strafing. The group did not begin flying P-51s in combat until the next month.[1]

The mission report also notes that the group sank the destroyer that day in the Adriatic Sea near Trieste. The pilots on the mission undoubtedly believed that they had sunk a German destroyer at that place and time. In a 2001 interview, Tuskegee Airman Lee Archer claimed that "we sank a destroyer escort," and when others doubted, "we sent them the film," implying that gun camera film showed the ship sinking.[2]

It is not likely that gun camera film, activated when the machine guns were fired, also showed the actual sinking of the ship, which would not have been immediate. Moreover, other records show that the only German ship that was attacked at the same place and time was the TA-22, the former World War I Italian destroyer *Giuseppe Missori*, which the Germans had converted into a very large torpedo vessel. The same records show that the ship did not sink on June 25, 1944, but was heavily damaged. The TA-22 was decommissioned on November 8, 1944, and scuttled at Trieste in May 1945. It might as well have been sunk on June 25, 1944, because it never fought the Allies again.[3]

The book *The Tuskegee Airmen* by Charles Francis notes that the Tuskegee Airmen attacked an enemy ship on June 25, 1944, and that Gwynne W. Pierson and Wendell O. Pruitt each earned a Distinguished Flying Cross for the mission. The book also claims that Pierson was given credit for sinking the ship. The only Distinguished Flying Cross I found for Gwynne W. Pierson was for his action on August 14, 1944 (Fifteenth Air Force General Order 287 dated January 19, 1945), and the only Distinguished Flying Cross I found for

Wendell O. Pruitt was for his action on August 27, 1944 (Fifteenth Air Force General Order 3950 dated October 15, 1944).[4]

Some sources suggest that the Tuskegee Airmen sank the German ship TA-27, which had been the Italian warship *Aurige*. The TA-27 was actually sunk on June 9, 1944, off the coast of Elba, west of the Italian peninsula, far from the Adriatic Sea, which is east of the Italian peninsula. The Tuskegee Airmen would not have sunk the TA-27, because the date and place do not match the group mission report.[5]

6

The misconception of the "Great Train Robbery"

One of the popular stories about the Tuskegee Airmen is sometimes nicknamed the "Great Train Robbery." According to the story, personnel in charge of supplying the 332d Fighter Group robbed a train to obtain unusually large 110-gallon wing tanks the group needed to fly the unusually long Berlin mission of March 24, 1945. The story goes on to say that the fuel tanks acquired had been designed to fit the P-47s, not the P-51 airplanes of the 332d Fighter Group, forcing the maintenance personnel to improvise the connections. According to the story, the maintainers were able to jury-rig the connections just in time for all the planes to be equipped to fly the Berlin mission.[1]

Another version of the story claims that only the 100th Fighter Squadron needed the larger tanks and that at night Capt. Omar Blair gathered a few enlisted men to seize the 110-gallon tanks from a train moving from Naples to deliver them to another group. As the story goes, the men "commandeered six flatbed trucks" and used one to block the tracks so that the train would have to stop. Using submachine guns, they then forced "the shocked white staff sergeants operating the train" to give them the 110-gallon fuel tanks they needed. Using the six trucks, Blair's group delivered the larger tanks just in time for the 332d Fighter Group to fly the Berlin mission.[2]

There are reasons to question the popular versions of the story. The larger 110-gallon fuel tanks were not new to the 332d Fighter Group. In fact, they had been used on the longer missions of the group for weeks before March 1945.[3] The group would not have needed to modify the tanks to fit the P-51 aircraft, since the P-51s had carried such tanks before. James Sheppard was a crew chief in the 301st Fighter Squadron and took part in preparing a P-51 of the 332d Fighter Group for the March 24, 1945, mission to Berlin during the night before the mission. As an experienced aircraft maintenance technician, he did not experience any difficulty in mounting larger fuel tanks to the wings of the P-51 he was maintaining so that they could carry out the mission.[4]

A version of the misconception includes the claim that the larger fuel tanks the 332d Fighter Group obtained the night before the Berlin mission were made for P-47 airplanes and had to be hastily adapted to fit the wings of P-51s.[5] A version of the story is that the Tuskegee Airmen mechanics armed themselves just before the Berlin mission to raid the bases of P-47 units to steal

TABLE 7 • 110-Gallon Fuel Tanks on Hand, 332d Fighter Group

Week Ending 1945	Air Service Squadron	Fighter Group	Base	110-Gallon Fuel Tanks on Hand
February 2	366	332	Ramitelli	563
February 9	366	332	Ramitelli	424
February 16	366	332	Ramitelli	295
February 23	366	332	Ramitelli	48
March 2	366	332	Ramitelli	Not given
March 9	366	332	Ramitelli	187
March 16	366	332	Ramitelli	0
March 23	366	332	Ramitelli	0
March 30	366	332	Ramitelli	64

Sources: February and March 1945 histories of the 38th Air Service Group.

the larger fuel tanks of those other fighter planes, and then they jury-rigged the stolen tanks to fit the Tuskegee Airmen P-51s so that they would have the range to go all the way to Berlin and back.[6] That is absurd. None of the fighter groups of the Fifteenth Air Force in Italy had flown P-47 airplanes since early July 1944.[7] In fact, the last of the groups to ever fly P-47s was the Tuskegee Airmen's 332d Fighter Group. Eight months had passed since P-47s were used by the fighter escorts in the Mediterranean Theater. The idea that 110-gallon fuel tanks for P-47s were being shipped to the Foggia area by train in March 1945 makes no sense, since P-47s had not been used by the fighter escorts in the theater for many months.

The 332d Fighter Group was not the only P-51 fighter escort group to fly the Berlin mission. There were three other P-51 groups that flew the same mission, and they also used the larger fuel tanks to reach the target and get back. Two of the P-51 groups, the 31st and the 325th Fighter Groups, had an ample supply of the 110-gallon fuel tanks in the latter half of March 1945. Two of the others, the 52d and the 332d Fighter Groups, ran out of the larger tanks in mid-March 1945, just before the mission.[8] Apparently, they had to go to extraordinary lengths to get the fuel tanks they needed.

TABLE 8 • Transition of Fifteenth Air Force Fighter Groups from P-47s to P-51s

Fighter Group	Last Month Flying P-47s	First Month Flying P-51s
325	May 1944	May 1944
332	June 1944	July 1944

Source: Maurer Maurer, Air Force Combat Units of World War II (Washington, D.C.: Office of Air Force History, 1983).

On March 23, 1945, the 55th Air Service Squadron of the 380th Air Service Group dispatched trucks from the depot at Foggia to the railhead at Chieuti for the larger fuel tanks. The squadron's diary entry for March 24, 1945, notes that it received "one trailer load of 110 gal auxiliary tanks for 366th Air Service Squadron." The 366th Air Service Squadron was based at Ramitelli, Italy, with the 332d Fighter Group, to service its P-51 aircraft. Another 55th Air Service Squadron diary entry in March 1945 notes that the squadron also used trucks to deliver 110-gallon fuel tanks from Chieuti to the 52d Fighter Group, which, like the 332d Fighter Group, flew P-51s for the Fifteenth Air Force and was based near Ramitelli.[9] The larger 110-gallon auxiliary fuel tanks were delivered to Ramitelli by truck, not from the depot at Foggia, where the smaller fuel tanks had been obtained, but from a railhead at Chieuti instead. At least some of the fuel tanks the 332d Fighter Group used for the mission came from Chieuti, and from the 55th Air Service Squadron, which shared them with the 366th Air Service Squadron at Ramitelli. Those tanks were not stolen from a train but were rather obtained from a railhead.

A version of the "Great Train Robbery" legend notes that personnel of the 523d Air Service Group scrounged up the 110-gallon tanks.[10] One of the problems with this account is that the 523d Air Service Group was not active until April 4, 1945, almost two weeks after the Berlin mission.[11]

According to Tuskegee Airman Lee Archer, who told a version of what he called "The Great Train Robbery" story in an interview with Dr. Lisa Bratton in March 2001 in New York, when larger fuel tanks were needed for the Berlin mission, which was farther than other missions, "our enlisted men, under a warrant officer, went to the depot and took 'em." Archer's version of the story contradicts other versions, which suggest that a train was actually stopped and robbed instead of a depot.[12]

The day after the Berlin mission, Col. Benjamin O. Davis Jr., commander of the 332d Fighter Group, commended Capt. Omar Blair of the 366th Air Service Squadron for his part in obtaining the fuel tanks the 332d Fighter Group needed for the Berlin mission. Capt. Blair subsequently also commended S. Sgt. George Watson of the squadron for leading a detail that traveled sixty miles to obtain the wing tanks needed for the all-important Berlin mission. The letters of commendation noted that the efforts were undertaken the evening of March 23 and the predawn hours of March 24, just in time for the mission to succeed. Capt. Blair and S. Sgt. Watson were instrumental in the success of the 332d Fighter Group's part in the longest Fifteenth Air Force air raid of the war, but the story that they had to rob a train, and that the 110-gallon fuel tanks had to be jury-rigged to fit the P-51s, is not consistent with the historical records.[13]

7

The misconception of superiority

....

A popular story circulating about the Tuskegee Airmen is that while many expected the "Tuskegee Airmen experiment" to prove that black pilots were inferior to white pilots and that the black pilots would fail, the Tuskegee Airmen actually proved the opposite: that they were superior to the white pilots and significantly outperformed them.[1] Whether the 332d Fighter Group was better or worse than the other three P-51 groups in the Fifteenth Air Force is debatable.

By May 1947, Col. Noel F. Parrish was a student at the Air Command and Staff School at Maxwell Air Force Base, after having served as commander of the basic and advanced flying school at Tuskegee Army Air Field, and commander of that station, for about five years. During that time, he had become an enemy of racial segregation within the Army Air Forces, and he wrote a thesis to explain why. A quote from that thesis is instructive: "Each establishment of a 'Negro unit' project was finally covered with a smoke screen of praise which clouded the issues and obscured the facts."[2] In another part of the same thesis, Parrish noted that the black units "gathered more than necessary praise" and that "military men showed an overwhelming tendency to believe, repeat, and exaggerate all the stories." He commented, "Such a situation [segregation] leads to an exaggeration of both the honors and the defamations." Philosophically, he wrote "when it is difficult to tell which praise is merited, it is certainly difficult to determine what blame is deserved."[3] Having been deeply involved in the training of Tuskegee Airmen pilots and having kept up with their performance during World War II, Parrish was aware that there were some misconceptions regarding what they did and did not actually accomplish. He was unquestionably supporting of their success, but he opposed segregation, preferring that black servicemembers be integrated into the Army Air Forces instead.

The number of bombers under Tuskegee Airmen escort that were shot down by enemy aircraft was twenty-seven, but the average number of bombers under the escort of white fighter groups in the Fifteenth Air Force, in the same time period, was forty-six.[4] The numbers suggest that the 332d Fighter Group lost significantly fewer bombers than the white fighter groups and therefore outperformed them. A related claim is that the 332d Fighter Group developed such a reputation for superior escort performance that the bombardment groups requested to be escorted by the "Red Tails" rather than the other fighter escort groups.

A popular story is that the black pilots of the 332d Fighter Group were the only fighter escort pilots to stay with the bombers they were assigned to protect and that the white fighter pilots of the other groups invariably left the bombers to go after enemy fighters to shoot down, in order to build up their totals of aerial victory credits. One version of this story appears in Kai Wright's book *Soldiers of Freedom: An Illustrated History of African Americans in the Armed Forces*: "Throughout the war, it [the 332d Fighter Group] flew bomber escorts—duty rejected by white pilots because it didn't offer as much opportunity to earn kills, and thus praise and promotion—and earned a reputation as the Air Force's most reliable escort."[5]

The practice of fighter escorts "sticking with the bombers" was not unique to the 332d Fighter Group. The Eighth Air Force in England practiced the policy of staying with the bombers at least until early January 1944, when Lt. Gen. Jimmy Doolittle succeeded Maj. Gen. Ira Eaker as its commander. He ordered his VIII Fighter Command leader, Maj. Gen. William E. Kepner, to take down a sign saying the first duty of the fighter pilots was to bring back the bombers safely and replace it with another sign saying that the first duty of the fighter pilots was to shoot down enemy airplanes. Doolittle authorized his fighter escorts to leave the bombers and go after the enemy fighters.[6]

When Doolittle became commander of the Eighth Air Force, Lt. Gen. Eaker moved to the Mediterranean Theater and became commander of the Mediterranean Allied Air Forces, which supervised the Twelfth and Fifteenth Air Forces and British air forces in the Mediterranean theater. Eaker probably took his "stick with the bombers" policy with him, and it was the policy not only of the 332d Fighter Group but also of the other fighter escort groups in the Fifteenth Air Force.

The history of the Fifteenth Air Force covering November 1943–May 1945, volume 1, notes that "before the summer of 1944, the fighters always maintained close escort. The original policy of the Air Force, in fact, stipulated that the fighters were never to leave the bombers in order to make an attack unless enemy aircraft were obviously preparing to strike at the bomber formation. As enemy fighter opposition declined, however, one squadron, at the discretion of the group commander, was sometimes detached for a fighter sweep against the enemy. This was done on withdrawal only, and in no case before the bombers had reached the target"[7]

This document also notes that "during the counter-air campaign early in 1944, a particularly high level of efficiency was reached by the escort fighters. On four consecutive days in February, heavy bomber penetrations into Germany were covered by an escort of P-38s and P-47s. Bomber pilots reported that the cover provided on these missions was the best ever furnished in the Air Force up to that time." The May 1944 history of the 52d Fighter Group, written after that white fighter group had transitioned to P-51 Mustang fighters, notes that "the B-24 combat crews are highly pleased with the excellent escort work our group has been doing."[8] It bears noting that the 332d Fighter Group had not started to escort Fifteenth Air Force bombers yet. The 332d Fighter Group started escorting bombers for the Fifteenth Air Force on June 7, 1944. From this important document, it seems clear that the policy of the Fifteenth Air Force in the Mediterranean Theater of Operations, unlike the policy of the Eighth Air Force in England after Lt. Gen. James Doolittle took charge of it, was to furnish close escort for the bombers, not leaving them to go after enemy fighters in the distance, and that the bomber crews were pleased with the escort that had been provided by the white fighter groups. Apparently the 332d Fighter Group was not the only fighter group providing close escort in the Fifteenth Air Force and doing it well enough for the bomber crews to express appreciation.[9]

None of the twenty-one heavy bomber groups in the Fifteenth Air Force was stationed at the same airfield as any of the seven fighter groups.[10] The assignments rotated, and one fighter group was not always assigned to escort the same bombardment wing or wings, or to provide the same kind of escort day after day. For example, sometimes a group would be assigned penetration escort, sometimes withdrawal escort, sometimes escort over the target, and sometimes a combination of them. The daily mission reports show that all the groups were flying the same kinds of missions, for the most part, and do not indicate that only one was escorting effectively. On many days, more than one fighter group was escorting many bomber groups heading for the same target. Because the assignments were made on a rotational basis by headquarters, apparently without discrimination, the idea that bombardment crews could request one fighter group over another for escort duty, and get it, is not likely. All of the bombardment groups were stationed at bases miles away from the 332d Fighter Group at Ramitelli Air Field in Italy, and their personnel had little or no interaction with the personnel of the fighter groups that escorted them. Most of them did not have the option of choosing one group over another.

TABLE 9 • Stations of Fifteenth Air Force Groups, June 1944–May 1945

Group	Wing	Airfield	Predominate Aircraft Type
2 Bombardment	5 Bombardment	Amendola, Italy	B-17
97 Bombardment	5 Bombardment	Amendola, Italy	B-17
99 Bombardment	5 Bombardment	Tortorella, Italy	B-17
301 Bombardment	5 Bombardment	Lucera, Italy	B-17
463 Bombardment	5 Bombardment	Celone, Italy	B-17
483 Bombardment	5 Bombardment	Sterparone, Italy	B-17
98 Bombardment	47 Bombardment	Lecce, Italy	B-24
376 Bombardment	47 Bombardment	San Pancrazio, Italy	B-24
449 Bombardment	47 Bombardment	Grottaglie, Italy	B-24
450 Bombardment	47 Bombardment	Manduria, Italy	B-24
451 Bombardment	49 Bombardment	Castelluccio, Italy	B-24
461 Bombardment	49 Bombardment	Torretto, Italy	B-24
484 Bombardment	49 Bombardment	Torretto, Italy	B-24
460 Bombardment	55 Bombardment	Spinazzola, Italy	B-24
464 Bombardment	55 Bombardment	Pantanella, Italy	B-24
465 Bombardment	55 Bombardment	Pantanella, Italy	B-24
485 Bombardment	55 Bombardment	Venosa, Italy	B-24
454 Bombardment	304 Bombardment	San Giovanni, Italy	B-24
455 Bombardment	304 Bombardment	San Giovanni, Italy	B-24
456 Bombardment	304 Bombardment	Stornara, Italy	B-24
459 Bombardment	304 Bombardment	Giulia, Italy	B-24
1 Fighter	305 Fighter	Salsola, then Vincenzo, then Salsola, then Lesina, Italy	P-38
14 Fighter	305 Fighter	Triolo, Italy	P-38
82 Fighter	305 Fighter	Vincenzo, Italy	P-38
31 Fighter	306 Fighter	San Severo, then Mondolfo, Italy	P-51
52 Fighter	306 Fighter	Madna, then Piagiolino, Italy	P-51
325 Fighter	306 Fighter	Lesina, then Rimini, then Mondolfo, Italy	P-51
332 Fighter	306 Fighter	Ramitelli, Italy	P-47 and P-51

Source: Maurer Maurer, Air Force Combat Units of World War II *(Washington, D.C.: Office of Air Force History, 1983).*

At least one of the bombardment groups had become acquainted with the 332d Fighter Group and knew it consisted of black pilots flying bomber escort duty. On December 29, 1944, eighteen B-24 bombers were forced by bad weather to land at Ramitelli Air Field in Italy, the home base of the 332d Fighter Group, which was flying P-51s. Seventeen of those bombers came from the 485th Bombardment Group, and the other one came from the 455th Bombardment Group. Most of the white bomber crews spent five days with the Tuskegee Airmen, enjoying their hospitality at a very crowded base. The 332d Fighter Group left a note in each bomber noting that the 332d Fighter Group's red-tailed escort fighters were there to protect them on their bombing missions. If any bomber crews requested that the 332d Fighter Group escort them, they probably belonged to the 485th or 455th Bombardment Groups, some of whose personnel had met members of the 332d Fighter Group and shared accommodations with them. The request would have been based on the bomber crews' experience at Ramitelli and not because the 332d Fighter Group had demonstrated its obvious superiority to the other fighter groups of the Fifteenth Air Force.[11]

At times, the bombardment crews would mistake one set of escorts for another. For example, World War II B-24 bomber pilot John Sonneborn remembered gratefully that his aircraft was saved by a red-tailed P-51 pilot when he was flying a mission to Ploesti, Romania, on May 5, 1944. He assumed that he had been escorted by a Tuskegee Airman, since he learned after the war that they had flown red-tailed P-51s in his theater. What Mr. Sonneborn did not realize was that the 332d Fighter Group did not begin flying missions to escort heavy bombers such as B-24s until June 1944, and the 332d Fighter Group did not begin flying P-51 aircraft until July 1944. If Sonneborn were saved by a pilot in a red-tailed P-51, that fighter pilot must have belonged to the 31st Fighter Group, because the 31st Fighter Group escorted B-24s to Ploesti on May 5, 1944, and the tails of the 31st Fighter Group P-51s were painted with red stripes. After the war, bomber crews sometimes gave fighter escort credit to the wrong group.[12]

Another example is a January 1, 2014, article titled "Tuskegee Airmen Assured Fellow Pilots a Happy New Year," by Pete Mecca, published in the *Covington News* of Newton County, Georgia. The article notes that Jim Shreib in a B-24 bomber was escorted home by a Tuskegee Airman in a red-tailed P-51 on November 14, 1944. The problem is that the 332d Fighter Group, to which the Red Tails belonged at the time, did not fly a mission on November 14, 1944. The group prepared a narrative mission report for each mission they flew for the Fifteenth Air Force, and the reports are numbered sequentially. On

November 11, 1944, the group flew mission 118, and on November 16, 1944, the group flew mission 119. The Tuskegee Airmen's 332d Fighter Group did not fly any missions from November 12 to 15, 1944. If Shreib was escorted by a pilot in a red-tailed P-51 on November 14, 1944, that pilot must have belonged to the 31st Fighter Group, which flew P-51s with red-striped tails.[13]

Yet the statistics still suggest strongly that the Tuskegee Airmen lost significantly fewer bombers to enemy aircraft fire than the average number lost by the other fighter groups in the Fifteenth Air Force. Does that mean the Tuskegee Airmen were superior?

One measure of the quality of the fighter escort groups was not just the number of bombers they lost to enemy aircraft fire but the number of enemy fighters they destroyed, because each of those enemy fighters was a potential bomber killer. Shooting down enemy fighters was also a way to protect the bombers. In November 1945, the War Department published a report titled "Policy for Utilization of Negro Manpower in the Post-War Army." Since the report had been prepared by a committee of generals headed by Lt. Gen. Alvan C. Gillem Jr., it was sometimes called the "Gillem Report." Part of the report compared the four P-51 fighter escort groups of the Fifteenth Air Force, which included the all-black 332d Fighter Group and the all-white 31st, 52d, 325th, and 332d Fighter Groups (the other three fighter escort groups of the Fifteenth Air Force, the 1st, 14th, and 82d, flew P-38 aircraft). While the report praised the 332d Fighter Group for successfully escorting bombers, it also criticized the group for having fewer aerial victory credits than the other groups because it did not aggressively chase enemy fighters to shoot them down. The report also claimed that each of the three white P-51 fighter groups shot down more than twice as many aircraft as it lost in combat but that the 332d Fighter Group lost more of its own aircraft in combat than it destroyed of the enemy.

A comparison of the aerial victory credits of the seven fighter groups of the Fifteenth Air Force covering the period the 332d Fighter Group flew for

TABLE 10 · Comparison of Fifteenth Air Force P-51 Fighter Groups

Fighter Group	Predominant Race	Victories per Aircraft Lost in Combat
31st	White	2.49
52d	White	2.08
325th	White	2.22
332d	Black	0.66

Source: "Policy for Utilization of Negro Manpower in the Post-War Army," Report of War Department Special Board on Negro Manpower, November 1945, AFHRA, call number 170.2111-1, November 1945), section on historical evaluation of the Negro's Military Service, subsection 9, evaluation of combat performance of the Negro in World War II, under g., "combat aviation,"[15].

TABLE 11 • Fighter Aces of the Fifteenth Air Force by Group, June 1944–April 1945

Fighter Group	Fighter Squadrons	Aircraft Type Flown	Number of Aces
1	27, 71, 94	P-38	2
14	37, 48, 49	P-38	1
82	95, 96, 97	P-38	4
31	307, 308, 309	P-51	10
52	2, 4, 5	P-51	10
325	317, 318, 319	P-51	11
332	99, 100, 301, 302	P-47 and P-51*	0

Sources: Maurer Maurer, Air Force Combat Units of World War II (Washington, D.C.: Office of Air Force History, 1983), for squadrons of each group and aircraft flown by each group; USAF Historical Study No. 85, USAF Credits for the Destruction of Enemy Aircraft, World War II (Washington, D.C.: Office of Air Force History, 1978), for aerial victory credits for each squadron listed chronologically; Barrett Tillman email to Daniel Haulman, May 23, 2012.

* The 332d Fighter Group obtained its P-51 aircraft in July 1944.

the Fifteenth Air Force, between early June 1944 and the end of the war in Europe in May 1945, reveals that each of the groups, except the 332d Fighter Group, produced at least one ace. The three groups that flew P-38 aircraft each produced only one or two aces in the period considered, but each of the three P-51 groups, besides the 332d Fighter Group, had at least ten. In other words, during the period June 1944 through the end of the war in Europe, each of the P-51 fighter groups of the Fifteenth Air Force, except the 332d Fighter Group, had at least ten pilots who each shot down at least five enemy aircraft. The 332d Fighter Group had none. The 31st and 52d Fighter Groups each had ten, and the 325th Fighter Group had eleven.[14]

Why was the 332d Fighter Group the only one of the Fifteenth Air Force P-51 groups that had no pilots to shoot down at least five enemy aircraft when the other three such groups each had at least ten such pilots? There are a number of possible explanations. The 332d Fighter Group, of all the P-51 groups in the Fifteenth Air Force, shot down the least number of enemy aircraft, and the fewer the number of aircraft shot down, the less the chances for the pilots to become aces. Another possible reason is that the 332d Fighter Group had more P-51 pilots on any given mission, since that group had four squadrons, and the other groups had only three. More pilots in the group meant less opportunity for each of the pilots to become an ace. The members of the 332d Fighter Group might have performed more as a team, with no pilot attempting to become a superstar at the expense of the others or of the bombers they were protecting. Another theory, already addressed in a previous misconception regarding Lee Archer, is that there was a racial conspiracy to prevent a black man from becoming an ace. As already mentioned, there is no documentation to support that theory, and the documentation that does exist contradicts it. Another explanation is that Col. Benjamin O. Davis Jr., commander of the 332d Fighter Group, would not allow his fighter pilots to leave the bombers in order to chase enemy fighters and build up their aerial victory credit claims and scores.

In comparing the 332d Fighter Group with the other P-51 fighter groups of the Fifteenth Air Force between June 1944 and the end of April 1945, when they were all primarily escorting bombers, one should bear in mind two factors. The more enemy aircraft a group encountered, the greater the chance the group had to shoot down enemy airplanes, and the less chance the enemy had to shoot down escorted bombers. If the 332d Fighter Group encountered fewer enemy aircraft than the other groups, it would have had less opportunity to shoot down enemy aircraft, and enemy aircraft would have had less opportunity to shoot down escorted bombers. Another factor to consider is the fact that the 332d Fighter Group was the last one to be assigned to the Fifteenth Air Force. Its pilots did not have as much experience as the pilots of the other groups in aerial combat associated with long-range escort missions, at least during June and July 1944. In addition to that, during June and July 1944, unlike the other groups, the 332d Fighter Group and its squadrons were transitioning from P-39 to P-47 aircraft, and from P-40 and P-47 aircraft to P-51 aircraft. By the time the 332d Fighter Group pilots were used to flying P-51s and engaging enemy aircraft challenging the bomber formations, the enemy aircraft opposition had declined considerably. By the latter half of 1944 and the first half of 1945, the German Air Force was a shadow of its former self, and the majority of the bomber escort missions encountered no enemy aircraft.

Members of the 332d Fighter Group encountered enemy aircraft on only 35 of their 179 bomber escort missions for the Fifteenth Air Force (they flew a total of 312 missions for the Fifteenth Air Force between early June 1944 and late April 1945, but many of the missions did not escort bombers). They shot down enemy aircraft on only twenty-one of those missions. Members of the 332d Fighter Group lost escorted bombers to enemy aircraft on only seven of their Fifteenth Air Force missions.[15]

In the final analysis, whether the Tuskegee Airmen were superior or inferior to the other fighter escort groups with which they served depends on the criteria. On one hand, the Tuskegee Airmen seemed to be superior because they lost significantly fewer escorted bombers to enemy aircraft than the average fighter group in the Fifteenth Air Force. On the other hand, the Tuskegee Airmen seemed to be inferior because they shot down fewer enemy fighters than any other P-51 fighter group in the Fifteenth Air Force. I prefer to conclude that the Tuskegee Airmen proved, by their exemplary combat performance, not that they were superior or inferior to the white fighter pilots, but that they were equal to them. The issue is not really superiority or inferiority, but equality. Furthermore, each pilot should really be measured as an individual, not as part of some artificial class. There were unquestionably some individual black fighter pilots who had superior records than some individual white fighter pilots, and vice versa.

8

The misconception that the Tuskegee Airmen units were all black

By the time the Tuskegee Airmen fighter squadrons and groups deployed overseas during World War II, they were all black. It is tempting to think that all the Tuskegee Airmen organizations always consisted of all black personnel, but they did not begin that way. Originally, white officers held the highest positions in those organizations and remained in some of those organizations as late as the summer of 1945.

The most famous of the Tuskegee Airmen military organizations were the 99th Fighter Squadron, the first black flying unit in the American military; the 332d Fighter Group, the first black fighter group; and the 477th Bombardment Group, the first black bomber group. All of these Tuskegee Airmen military organizations began with both black and white members. The first three commanders of the 99th Fighter Squadron (originally called the 99th Pursuit Squadron) were white. They were Capt. Harold R. Maddux, 2d Lt. Clyde H. Bynum, and Capt. Alonzo S. Ward. The first two commanders of the 332d Fighter Group were white. They were Lt. Col. Sam W. Westbrook and Col. Robert R. Selway. The first commander of the 477th Bombardment Group after it was activated as a predominantly black group was white. He was Col. Robert R. Selway (who had earlier commanded the 332d Fighter Group). All of these military organizations eventually became all-black, but they did not begin this way.[1]

The 96th Service Group, later called the 96th Air Service Group, which serviced the aircraft of the Tuskegee Airmen fighter units, is also considered a Tuskegee Airmen organization. It was first activated at Tuskegee Army Air Field. Unlike the 332d Fighter Group and its squadrons, which were all black by the time they deployed overseas, the 96th Service Group continued to have white officers within its ranks even during the time it served in Italy.[2]

Many of the flight instructors at Tuskegee were white. This was true at all three of the bases around Tuskegee, including Kennedy Field, where civilian pilot training took place; at Moton Field, where the primary flight training occurred; and at Tuskegee Army Air Field, where the basic, advanced, and transition training was completed. White officers retained leadership positions in the flight-training organizations at Moton Field and Tuskegee Army Air Field throughout World War II. While the majority of flight instructors at Moton Field were black, the majority of the flight instructors at Tuskegee Army Air Field remained white.[3]

For more than a year before the 99th Fighter Squadron was assigned to the 332d Fighter Group, it served in combat overseas while attached to various white fighter groups, as if it were one of the squadrons of those groups. In effect, those groups included both black and white personnel while the 99th Fighter Squadron was attached to them. Some of the members of the 99th Fighter Squadron, which by then had become an all-black organization, resented being assigned to the 332d Fighter Group, because they had become accustomed to serving in white groups, flying alongside white fighter squadrons, and did not relish being placed with the black fighter group simply because they were also black. In a sense, it was a step back toward more segregation. At any rate, many Tuskegee Airmen during World War II served in units that once included white personnel, although as the war progressed, most of their organizations became all black.[4]

Some of the white officers who were in command of Tuskegee Airmen opposed equal opportunities for them. Col. William Momyer of the 33d Fighter Group opposed the continued combat role of the 99th Fighter Squadron when it was attached to his group, and Col. Robert Selway, commander of the 477th Bombardment Group at Freeman Field, attempted to enforce segregated officers' clubs at that base, and had many of the Tuskegee Airmen arrested for opposing his policy.[5] But for every white officer who discouraged equal opportunity for the Tuskegee Airmen under their command, there were other white officers who sincerely worked for their success. They included Forrest Shelton, who instructed pilots in civilian and primary pilot training at Kennedy and Moton Fields near Tuskegee; Maj. William T. Smith, who supervised primary pilot training at Moton Field; Capt. Robert M. Long, a flight instructor who taught the first Tuskegee Airmen pilots to graduate from advanced pilot training at Tuskegee Army Air Field; Col. Noel Parrish, commander of the pilot training at Tuskegee Army Air Field; and Col. Earl E. Bates, commander of the 79th Fighter Group for most of the time the 99th Fighter Squadron was attached to it (from October 1943 to April 1944).[6]

Even the black pilots of the Tuskegee Airmen units were not all black. Many of them descended not only from African Americans but also from European Americans and Native Americans. Some were a mixture of all three. Yet no matter how little African American blood they had, most of the members of the Tuskegee Airmen organizations were classified as being "colored" in the World War II period. The skin colors, hair textures, and facial features of the Tuskegee Airmen varied as greatly as their height. Some of the Tuskegee Airman pilots looked more white than black. The racial diversity among the members of the Tuskegee Airmen organizations belied the foolish idea that men should be separated from each other on the basis of what they looked like. One Tuskegee Airman, Eugene Smith, was not black at all but rather of European and Native American heritage. The doctor that delivered him wrote "colored" on his birth certificate. Because of that label, Smith could fly for the Army Air Forces only if he went to Tuskegee, and so he did.[7]

9

The misconception that all Tuskegee Airmen were fighter pilots who flew red-tailed P-51s to escort bombers

Museum displays, World War II history books, magazine articles, pamphlets, newspaper articles, television programs, and even movies sometimes describe only one part of the Tuskegee Airmen story, misleading readers or observers into thinking that all the Tuskegee Airmen flew red-tailed P-51s on bomber escort missions deep into enemy territory. The Tuskegee Airmen's story is much more complex than that. In fact, the Tuskegee Airmen flew four kinds of fighter aircraft in combat, and also bombers not in combat. Many of the Tuskegee Airmen who flew in combat during World War II and earned distinguished records never saw a red-tailed P-51. A good example is Charles Dryden, who returned from Italy months before any of the Tuskegee Airmen flew any P-51s overseas, and months before they received the assignment to escort heavy bombers deep into enemy territory.[1]

To be sure, the most famous Tuskegee Airmen flew red-tailed P-51 Mustangs to escort Fifteenth Air Force heavy bombers on raids deep into enemy territory, but not all of them did so. Before July 1944, the 99th Fighter Squadron flew P-40 fighters on patrol and air-to-ground attack missions against enemy targets on tactical missions for the Twelfth Air Force. Sometimes these missions involved escorting medium bombers, but more often they involved supporting Allied surface forces and defending them from attack by enemy aircraft in Italy. During June 1944, the 332d Fighter Group flew P-47 aircraft on bomber escort missions. Before then, the group and its three fighter squadrons flew P-39 aircraft on tactical missions for the Twelfth Air Force, supporting Allied ground forces in Italy. Neither the P-39s nor the P-40s had red tails. In July 1944, the 99th Fighter Squadron was assigned to the 332d Fighter Group, and only in that month did the group begin to fly red-tailed P-51s. The group painted the tails of the aircraft red because the Fifteenth Air Force had seven fighter escort groups, including three P-38 and four P-51 groups. All four of the P-51 groups had distinctively painted tails. The 31st Fighter Group had red-striped tails; the 52d Fighter Group had yellow tails; the 325th Fighter Group had black and yellow checkerboard-patterned tails. The tails of the 332d Fighter Group were painted solid red.[2] The assigned colors for each group helped distinguish it from other groups in large formations flying to, from, and over enemy targets. The various colored tails also helped bomber crews tell which groups were escorting them and whether distant fighters were friend or foe.

Some of the African American pilots who trained at Tuskegee Army Air Field during World War II never became fighter pilots at all. They became bomber pilots, and after their Tuskegee training, were assigned to the 477th Bombardment Group, which flew twin-engined B-25s. This group never deployed overseas to take part in combat during the war.[3]

10

The misconception that after a flight with a black pilot at Tuskegee, Eleanor Roosevelt persuaded the president to establish a flying unit for African Americans in the Army Air Corps

....

Contrary to a persistent misconception, Eleanor Roosevelt's visit to Tuskegee Institute at the end of March 1941 did not result in her convincing her husband, President Franklin D. Roosevelt, to establish a black flying unit in the Army Air Corps.[1]

In fact, the decision to establish a black flying unit in the Army Air Corps had been announced by the War Department on January 16, 1941, more than two months before Eleanor Roosevelt's visit to Tuskegee. The announcement included mention of plans to train support personnel for the unit at Chanute Field, Illinois, followed by pilot training at Tuskegee. On March 19, 1941, the War Department constituted the first black flying unit, the 99th Pursuit Squadron, and on March 22, the unit was activated at Chanute Field.[2] A week after the 99th Pursuit Squadron was activated, Eleanor Roosevelt visited Tuskegee and was given an airplane ride over Tuskegee. The date was March 29, 1941.[3] The pilot was Charles Anderson, chief instructor who taught civilian pilot training at Tuskegee Institute. The President's wife visited Tuskegee, not to get a black flying squadron started, but because the black flying squadron had been started and was scheduled to move from Chanute to Tuskegee after its support personnel had been trained.

Eleanor Roosevelt undoubtedly supported the efforts to establish flight training for black servicemembers at Tuskegee, and her visit to Tuskegee Institute encouraged contributions for the building of a primary flying base at Tuskegee (which later became Moton Field), but she did not convince her husband to establish the first black flying unit after her flight with Chief Anderson at Tuskegee, because the 99th Pursuit Squadron had already been announced in January and constituted and activated before her Tuskegee visit.

Another aspect of the popular story about Eleanor Roosevelt riding with a black pilot at Tuskegee includes the notion that the Secret Service agents protecting her objected to her taking the flight with a black pilot because they were concerned about her safety, and that they called Washington, D.C., to see if it was okay with President Franklin D. Roosevelt. The president is said to have responded that they should let Eleanor do what she wanted. That part of the story is also questionable. Lewis Gould, in his book *American First Ladies, Their Lives and their Legacy*, noted that Eleanor Roosevelt "adamantly refused Secret Service protection" throughout the years her husband was president. If this is true, she would not have had Secret Service agents there at Tuskegee to object to her flying with a black pilot.[4]

11

The misconception that the Tuskegee Airmen earned 150 Distinguished Flying Crosses during World War II

For many years, the Tuskegee Airmen were said to have earned 150 Distinguished Flying Crosses during World War II. According to Dr. Roscoe Brown, an original Tuskegee Airmen who earned his own Distinguished Flying Cross (DFC), 150 is the usual number one hears or reads for DFCs that were earned by Tuskegee Airmen. He said the number was based on information from *The Tuskegee Airmen: The Men Who Changed a Nation* by Charles Francis. Francis noted that there was evidence for 95 DFCs awarded to Tuskegee Airmen, but possibly there were as many as 150.[1]

Craig Huntly of the Tuskegee Airmen Incorporated's Harry A. Sheppard Historical Research Committee checked all the Fifteenth Air Force general orders that awarded DFCs to Tuskegee Airmen and found that ninety-five had been awarded. He knew that the Tuskegee Airmen units in combat had also served with the Twelfth Air Force, before joining the Fifteenth Air Force, and that Twelfth Air Force general orders would also probably note additional DFCs awarded to Tuskegee Airmen. However, Huntly found only one Twelfth Air Force general order that awarded a DFC to a Tuskegee Airman. It recognized the aerial victory credit of Charles B. Hall, the first black pilot in military service to shoot down an enemy airplane. He found no other Twelfth Air Force orders that awarded DFCs to Tuskegee Airmen. Tuskegee Airmen who earned other aerial victory credits while flying with the Twelfth Air Force earned Air Medals instead of DFCs. The total number of DFCs awarded to Tuskegee Airmen was therefore ninety-six: ninety-five of which were awarded by Fifteenth Air Force orders, and one awarded by a Twelfth Air Force order. Moreover, one Tuskegee Airman, Capt. William A. Campbell, earned two DFCs. Therefore, ninety-five Tuskegee Airmen earned DFCs, but ninety-six DFCs were awarded to Tuskegee Airmen.

I searched through every one of the orders that Huntly listed and found the dates of the events for which each of the Tuskegee Airmen DFCs were awarded. I placed the events in chronological order so that I could include them in my larger Tuskegee Airmen Chronology. The correct number of

DFCs earned by the Tuskegee Airmen, for which there is documentation, is 96, not 150. Table 12 shows the numbers of all the 15th and Twelfth Air Force general orders that awarded DFCs to Tuskegee Airmen.

TABLE 12 • Chronological List of Tuskegee Airmen Distinguished Flying Cross Winners, by Date of the Action for Which Each DFC Was Awarded

Date	Name	Fighter Squadron of 332d Fighter Group	General Order Number and Date of Issue (All Issued by Fifteenth Air Force except First)
Jan. 28, 1944	Cpt. Charles B. Hall	99	64, May 22, 1944 (12 AF)
May 12, 1944	Cpt. Howard L. Baugh	99	4041, Oct. 19, 1944
May 21, 1944	1 Lt. Charles W. Tate	99	449, Jan. 31, 1945
May 27, 1944	1 Lt. Clarence W. Dart	99	449, Jan. 31, 1945
June 4, 1944	Cpt. Edward L. Toppins	99	4041, Oct. 19, 1944
June 4, 1944	Cpt. Leonard M. Jackson	99	4876, Dec. 5, 1944
June 5, 1944	Cpt. Elwood T. Driver	99	449, Jan. 31, 1945
June 9, 1944	Col. Benjamin O. Davis, Jr.	(332 Fighter Gp)	2972, Aug. 31, 1944
July 12, 1944	Cpt. Joseph D. Elsberry	301	2466, Aug. 10, 1944
July 16, 1944	Cpt. Alphonza W. Davis	(332 Fighter Gp)	3541, Sep. 22, 1944
July 16, 1944	1 Lt. William W. Green	302	49, Jan. 3, 1945
July 17, 1944	1 Lt. Luther H. Smith	302	5068, Dec. 18, 1944
July 17, 1944	1 Lt. Laurence D. Wilkins	302	49, Jan. 3, 1945
July 18, 1944	2 Lt. Clarence D. Lester	100	3167, Sep. 6, 1944
July 18, 1944	1 Lt. Jack D. Holsclaw	100	3167, Sep. 6, 1944
July 18, 1944	Cpt. Andrew D. Turner	100	4009, Oct. 17, 1944
July 18, 1944	1 Lt. Walter J. A. Palmer	100	654, Feb. 13, 1945
July 18, 1944	1 Lt. Charles P. Bailey	99	3484, May 29, 1945
July 20, 1944	Cpt. Henry B. Perry	99	4993, Dec. 14, 1944
July 25, 1944	Cpt. Harold E. Sawyer	301	4876, Dec. 5, 1944
July 27, 1944	1 Lt. Edward C. Gleed	(332 Fighter Gp)	3106, Sep. 4, 1944
Aug. 12, 1944	Cpt. Lee Rayford	301	5068, Dec. 18, 1944
Aug. 12, 1944	Cpt. Woodrow W. Crockett	100	49, Jan. 3, 1945
Aug. 12, 1944	Cpt. William T. Mattison	100	49, Jan. 3, 1945
Aug. 12, 1944	1 Lt. Freddie E. Hutchins	302	49, Jan. 3, 1945
Aug. 12, 1944	1 Lt. Lawrence B. Jefferson	301	49, Jan. 3, 1945
Aug. 12, 1944	1 Lt. Lowell C. Steward	100	231, Jan. 15, 1945
Aug. 14, 1944	Cpt. Melvin T. Jackson	302	3689, Sep. 29, 1944

Date	Name	Fighter Squadron of 332d Fighter Group	General Order Number and Date of Issue (All Issued by Fifteenth Air Force except First)
Aug. 14 1944	1 Lt. Gwynne W. Pierson	302	287, Jan. 19, 1945
Aug. 14, 1944	Cpt. Arnold W. Cisco	301	839, Feb. 21, 1945
Aug. 14, 1944	Cpt. Alton F. Ballard	301	1153, Mar. 5, 1945
Aug. 24, 1944	1 Lt. John F. Briggs	100	49, Jan. 3, 1945
Aug. 24, 1944	1 Lt. William H. Thomas	302	449, Jan. 31, 1945
Aug. 27, 1944	Cpt. Wendell O. Pruitt	302	3950, Oct. 15, 1944
Aug. 27, 1944	Cpt. Dudley M. Watson	302	4009, Oct. 17, 1944
Aug. 27, 1944	1 Lt. Roger Romine	302	5068, Dec. 18, 1944
Aug. 30, 1944	Cpt. Clarence H. Bradford	301	1811, Mar. 27, 1945
Sep. 8, 1944	Maj. George S. Roberts	(332 Fighter Gp)	137, Jan. 8, 1945
Sep. 8, 1944	1 Lt. Heber C. Houston	99	3484, May 29, 1945
Oct. 4, 1944	1 Lt. Samuel L. Curtis	100	158, Jan. 10, 1945
Oct. 4, 1944	1 Lt. Dempsey Morgan	100	231, Jan. 15, 1945
Oct. 4, 1944	Cpt. Claude B. Govan	301	255, Jan. 16, 1945
Oct. 4, 1944	1 Lt. Herman A. Lawson	99	449, Jan. 31, 1945
Oct. 4, 1944	1 Lt. Willard L. Woods	100	449, Jan. 31, 1945
Oct. 6, 1944	1 Lt. Alva N. Temple	99	231, Jan. 15, 1945
Oct. 6, 1944	Cpt. Lawrence E. Dickson	100	287, Jan. 19, 1945
Oct. 6, 1944	1 Lt. Edward M. Thomas	99	517, Feb. 6, 1945
Oct. 6, 1944	1 Lt. Robert L. Martin	100	839, Feb. 21, 1945
Oct. 6, 1944	Cpt. Robert J. Friend	301	1811, Mar. 27, 1945
Oct. 11, 1944	Cpt. William A. Campbell	99	4215, Oct. 28, 1944
Oct. 11, 1944	1 Lt. George E. Gray	99	4425, Nov. 10, 1944
Oct. 11, 1944	1 Lt. Felix J. Kirkpatrick	302	4876, Dec. 5, 1944
Oct. 11, 1944	1 Lt. Richard S. Harder	99	836, Feb. 21, 1945
Oct. 12, 1944	1 Lt. Lee Archer	302	4876, Dec. 5, 1944
Oct. 12, 1944	Cpt. Milton R. Brooks	302	255, Jan. 16, 1945
Oct. 12, 1944	1 Lt. Frank E. Roberts	100	287, Jan. 19, 1945
Oct. 12, 1944	1 Lt. Spurgeon N. Ellington	100	449, Jan. 31, 1945
Oct. 12, 1944	1 Lt. Leonard F. Turner	301	836, Feb. 21, 1945
Oct. 12, 1944	Cpt. Armour G. McDaniel	301	1430, Mar. 15, 1945
Oct. 12, 1944	Cpt. Stanley L. Harris	301	1811, Mar. 27, 1945

Continued

Date	Name	Fighter Squadron of 332d Fighter Group	General Order Number and Date of Issue (All Issued by Fifteenth Air Force except First)
Oct. 12, 1944	1 Lt. Marion R. Rodgers	99	1811, Mar. 27, 1945
Oct. 12, 1944	1 Lt. Quitman C. Walker	99	3484, May 29, 1945
Oct. 13, 1944	1 Lt. Milton S. Hays	99	719, Feb. 16, 1945
Oct. 14, 1944	1 Lt. George M. Rhodes, Jr.	100	49, Jan. 3, 1945
Oct. 21, 1944	Cpt. Vernon V. Haywood	302	5068, Dec. 18, 1944
Nov. 16, 1944	Cpt. Luke J. Weathers	302	5228, Dec. 28, 1944
Nov. 19, 1944	Cpt. Albert H. Manning	99	4876, Dec. 5, 1944
Nov. 19, 1944	Cpt. John Daniels	99	5068, Dec. 18, 1944
Nov. 19, 1944	1 Lt. William N. Alsbrook	99	836, Feb. 21, 1945
Nov. 19, 1944	1 Lt. Norman W. Scales	100	836, Feb. 21, 1945
Feb. 16, 1945	Cpt. Emile G. Clifton	99	3484, May 29, 1945
Feb. 17, 1945	Cpt. Louis G. Purnell	301	2362, Apr. 14, 1945
Feb. 25, 1945	1 Lt. Roscoe C. Brown	100	1430, Mar. 15, 1945
Feb. 25, 1945	1 Lt. Reid E. Thompson	100	2270, Apr. 11, 1945
Mar. 12, 1945	Cpt. Walter M. Downs	301	3484, May 29, 1945
Mar. 14, 1945	1 Lt. Shelby F. Westbrook	99	2362, Apr. 14, 1945
Mar. 14, 1945	1 Lt. Hannibal M. Cox	99	3031, May 5, 1945
Mar. 14, 1945	2 Lt. Vincent I. Mitchell	99	3031, May 5, 1945
Mar. 14, 1945	1 Lt. Thomas P. Braswell	99	3484, May 29, 1945
Mar. 14, 1945	2 Lt. John W. Davis	99	3484, May 29, 1945
Mar. 16, 1945	1 Lt. Roland W. Moody	301	2834, Apr. 28, 1945
Mar. 16, 1945	1 Lt. Henry R. Peoples	301	2834, Apr. 28, 1945
Mar. 16, 1945	1 Lt. William S. Price III	301	2834, Apr. 28, 1945
Mar. 24, 1945	1 Lt. Earl R. Lane	100	2834, Apr. 28, 1945
Mar. 24, 1945	2 Lt. Charles V. Brantley	100	2834, Apr. 28, 1945
Mar. 31, 1945	1 Lt. Robert W. Williams	100	3484, May 29, 1945
Mar. 31, 1945	1 Lt. Bertram W. Wilson Jr.	100	3484, May 29, 1945
Apr. 1, 1945	1 Lt. Charles L. White	301	2834, Apr. 28, 1945
Apr. 1, 1945	1 Lt. John E. Edwards	301	3484, May 29, 1945
Apr. 1, 1945	1 Lt. Harry T. Stewart Jr.	301	3484, May 29, 1945
Apr. 1, 1945	2 Lt. Carl E. Carey	301	3484, May 29, 1945
Apr. 15, 1945	Capt. Gordon M. Rapier	301	3324, May 21, 1945

Date	Name	Fighter Squadron of 332d Fighter Group	General Order Number and Date of Issue (All Issued by Fifteenth Air Force except First)
Apr. 15, 1945	1 Lt. Gentry E. Barnes	99	3484, May 29, 1945
Apr. 15, 1945	Cpt. William A. Campbell	99	3484, May 29, 1945
Apr. 15, 1945	1 Lt. Jimmy Lanham	301	3484, May 29, 1945
Apr. 26, 1945	1 Lt. Thomas W. Jefferson	301	3343, May 22, 1945

12

The misconception that the Tuskegee Airmen were the first to implement a "stick with the bombers" policy

In the *Red Tails* movie by George Lucas, released in January 2012, the Tuskegee Airmen appear to be the first fighter group to implement a "stick with the bombers" policy of fighter escort. All of the other fighter groups appear to be chasing after enemy fighters, leaving the bombers unprotected from other enemy fighters. That is not true. The "stick with the bombers" policy had been instituted by Maj. Gen. Ira Eaker when he was commander of the Eighth Air Force in England, long before the Tuskegee Airmen ever began heavy bomber escort. In January 1944, Eaker moved to the Mediterranean Theater of Operations, where the Tuskegee Airmen were to fly, and took his "stick with the bombers" ideas with him for the Fifteenth Air Force, over which he served as commander of the Mediterranean Allied Air Forces. At the same time, Lt. Gen. Jimmy Doolittle moved to England to take command of the Eighth Air Force. When he entered the office of the commander of the VIII Fighter Command, which managed the fighter escorts of the Eighth Air Force, he saw a sign that said: "The First Duty of the Eighth Air Force Fighters is to bring the bombers back alive." Doolittle ordered that the sign be taken down and declared that the first duty of the fighters is to destroy German fighters.[1]

When the Tuskegee Airmen followed a "stick with the bombers" escort policy, they were not implementing a brand-new policy but following the old policy of General Eaker. The fighter escorts of the Fifteenth Air Force under the Mediterranean Allied Air Forces refused to be lured away from the bombers they were protecting by enemy decoy fighters. That would have left the bombers more vulnerable to the other enemy fighters. The policy of going after the German fighters, instead of sticking with the bombers, was Doolittle's policy after he moved to England to take command of the Eighth Air Force early in 1944, but not the policy of the Fifteenth Air Force after General Eaker took command of the Mediterranean Allied Air Forces, under which the Fifteenth Air Force served.

13

The misconception that the 332d Fighter Group was the only one to escort Fifteenth Air Force bombers over Berlin

The *Red Tails* movie by George Lucas depicts the Berlin mission as if only two fighter groups were assigned to protect the Fifteenth Air Force bombers: the 52d and the 332d. In the movie, the 52d Fighter Group fails to show up, so the 332d Fighter Group stays with the bombers all the way to the target, being the only fighter group to protect the bombers on that mission. In a 2001 interview, Tuskegee Airman Lee Archer claimed that "the other group was supposed to relieve us got lost and didn't show up and our group decided that they would stay with the bombers."[1] In reality, the Fifteenth Air Force bombers that raided Berlin that day were protected by no less than five fighter groups, including not only the 52d and 332d, but also three other groups. Four of the fighter groups flew P-51s, and one flew P-38s. All of the five fighter groups flew all the way to Berlin to protect the bombers that day. In fact, whereas the 332d Fighter Group shot down three enemy jets that attacked the bombers near Berlin that day, the 31st Fighter Group shot down five in the same air battle.[2]

14

The misconception that the 99th Fighter Squadron, unlike the white fighter squadrons with which it served, at first flew obsolete P-40 airplanes

The Lucasfilm movie about the Tuskegee Airmen called *Red Tails* suggests that the Tuskegee Airmen, when flying their P-40s, were flying obsolete hand-me-down airplanes that the white units no longer flew. The 99th Fighter Squadron was the Tuskegee Airmen unit that flew P-40s in combat. When the 99th Fighter Squadron entered combat from bases first in north Africa, and later Sicily and still later on the mainland of Italy in 1943, it was flying the same kinds of aircraft as the P-40 groups to which it was attached in turn, and the same kinds of aircraft as the P-40 squadrons that were assigned to those same groups. If the P-40 was an obsolete aircraft, then groups to which it was attached, and the fighter squadrons assigned to those groups with which the 99th Fighter Squadron flew were also flying obsolete aircraft. In other words, if the P-40s were obsolete, many more white pilots were flying obsolete aircraft than black pilots.

Most of the time, the 99th Fighter Squadron was flying P-40s while attached to white P-40 groups, each of which had three other P-40 squadrons assigned, all the squadrons were flying the same kinds of missions. Those missions included attacking the enemy-held island of Pantelleria in the Mediterranean Sea, which surrendered without an invasion, and covering the Allied invasion of Sicily, to which the 99th Fighter Squadron moved with the group to which it was attached. In fact, both the group and the 99th Fighter Squadron earned a Distinguished Unit Citation for the missions against enemy-held Sicily. A Tuskegee Airman shot down an enemy aircraft exactly one month after the 99th Fighter Squadron flew its first combat mission. In truth, except for about a month in 1943, the 99th Fighter Squadron was not only flying the same kinds of aircraft, but also the same kinds of missions in the same areas, on the front lines facing the enemy.[1]

There is one exception. When the 33d Fighter Group and its three assigned P-40 squadrons moved from Sicily to mainland Italy on 13–14 September 1943, the 99th Fighter Squadron, also flying P-40s, remained back in Sicily, and stayed there until more than a month later, when it also moved to mainland Italy. During that month, the 99th Fighter Squadron was stationed far behind the squadrons assigned to the group, and therefore had much less opportunity to shoot down enemy aircraft. On October 16, 1943, the 99th Fighter Squadron was detached from the 33d Fighter Group and attached instead to the 79th Fighter Group. The next day, October 17, the 99th Fighter Squadron finally moved to the Italian mainland.[2]

The 99th Fighter Squadron earned two Distinguished Unit Citations before it was assigned to the 332d Fighter Group. If one reads the orders that awarded those honors, one would find no reference at all to the 99th Fighter Squadron. The honors were awarded to the 324th Fighter Group, for operations over Sicily in June and July 1943, and for operations over Cassino on 12–14 May 1944. The only reason the 99th Fighter Squadron also received the two Distinguished Unit Citations is because the 99th Fighter Squadron was attached to the 324th Fighter Group in June and July 1943 and again in May 1944. The 99th Fighter Squadron was flying the same aircraft (P-40s) on the same missions as the 324th Fighter Group. It was not flying an inferior aircraft, and most of the time, except between mid-September and mid-October 1943, it was not flying many miles away from the enemy, without the opportunity to excel in combat.[3]

At least two sources note that the 99th Fighter Squadron was flying better P-40s than the other P-40 squadrons in North Africa in 1943. Maj. Philip Cochran was a white officer in the 33d Fighter Group's 58th Fighter Squadron, who was ordered by Gen. Cannon to help train the pilots of the 99th Fighter Squadron in combat tactics and navigation. Cochran noted in an interview that the 99th Fighter Squadron had better equipment than the other squadrons, implying that the squadron was equipped with better P-40s.[4] Gail Buckley, in her book *American Patriots*, about blacks people in the military, also notes that the 99th Fighter Squadron had newer P-40s than the other squadrons in North Africa.[5] The idea that the 99th Fighter Squadron was flying planes more obsolete than the white fighter pilots had is only a myth.

Another aspect of the obsolete P-40 myth includes the notion that the P-40s the Tuskegee Airmen flew at first in combat were reconstructed from those actual P-40s that the Flying Tigers under Claire Chennault had flown in the China-Burma-India Theater. This version of the story claims that pieces of those aircraft were put together for the black pilots to use in North Africa, as if the remnants of those planes were the only P-40s the Army Air Forces had left.[6] The P-40s the 99th Fighter Squadron received in North Africa were new ones, according to the autobiography of Benjamin O. Davis, Jr. Not long after the 99th Fighter Squadron arrived in North Africa, it acquired "27 brand-new P-40Ls." The 99th Fighter Squadron did not fly old obsolete P-40s in combat.[7] The only older models it flew were back at Tuskegee during training.

15

The misconception that the training of black pilots for combat was an experiment designed to fail

....

Many publications about the Tuskegee Airmen claim that the program of training black pilots in the Army Air Forces was an experiment designed to fail, as if the Army Air Forces planned from the start to "wash out" all the pilot trainees before they had a chance to graduate, or that it planned from the start never to allow them to enter combat. The documentation from World War II does not support this claim, although there were many within the service, including some of the leading officers, who resisted the policy of granting black pilots the same opportunities as white pilots.

The World War II primary sources about the training of the black pilots at Moton Field and later at Tuskegee Army Air Field, and even at Selfridge Field, indicate that at least the local Army Air Forces officers by and large intended for the program to succeed. Studies by Robert "Jeff" Jakeman and J. Todd Moye prove that many Army Air Forces white personnel in the flight-training program for black pilots, with a few exceptions, worked for the success of the black pilots. The foremost Army Air Forces officer in charge of the black pilot training was Col. Noel Parrish. As commander of Tuskegee Army Air Field, where the pilots received their basic and advanced flight training and many of them also received their transition training, he had a vested interest in the success of the program. Many other white Army Air Forces officers took part in the training of black pilots, not only at Moton Field but also at Tuskegee Army Air Field. Among them were Maj. William T. Smith and Capt. Robert M. Long. Forrest Shelton was a white pilot who taught black pilots to fly both in civilian pilot training at Kennedy Field and in primary training at Moton Field. President Franklin D. Roosevelt, the commander in chief, had mandated the first black flying unit as early as 1940, and the War Department established and activated that unit in March 1941, even before any black pilots had been trained within the Army Air Forces. President Roosevelt and the Army Air Forces officers at Moton and Tuskegee Army Air Fields did not intend the program to fail.[1]

Even after the 99th Fighter Squadron deployed to North Africa to enter combat in the Mediterranean Theater of Operations, there were white officers who helped the squadron succeed. While the 33d Fighter Group commander, Col. William W. Momyer, attempted to remove the 99th Fighter Squadron from combat, or at least to remove it from attachment to his group, in 1943, not all white officers of the 33d Fighter Group were opponents of the 99th Fighter Squadron. One of them was Maj. Philip Cochran, who was ordered by Gen. John Cannon to help the newly arrived pilots of the 99th Fighter Squadron by training them in combat tactics and navigation, which Cochran did willingly.[2] Cochran was commander of the 33d Fighter Group's 58th Fighter Squadron. When the 99th Fighter Squadron was subsequently attached to the white 79th Fighter Group, its commander, Col. Earl E. Bates, welcomed the black squadron to his group and encouraged its success in combat, treating that squadron like the other three squadrons assigned to his group.[3]

16

The misconception of the hidden trophy

A popular story claims that when the Air Force held its first gunnery "Top Gun" meet in Las Vegas in 1949, the all-black 332d Fighter Group defeated all the other groups, but because a black group won, the competition was discontinued, and the trophy was hidden. Some sixty years later, the trophy was finally discovered, and the 332d Fighter Group was recognized for this unique achievement.[1]

In reality, the Air Force's 1949 gunnery meet in Las Vegas was not called "Top Gun," and the 332d Fighter Group was not the only fighter group to win. The 332d won the conventional (propeller-driven) aircraft category, while the 4th Fighter Group won the jet aircraft category. In 1950, the Air Force held another gunnery meet in Las Vegas, but by then, the all-black 332d Fighter Group had been inactivated. Two other organizations, the 3525th Aircraft Gunnery Squadron and the 27th Fighter Escort Group, won the 1950 gunnery meet, the first for the jet aircraft category, and the second for the conventional (propeller-driven) aircraft category. The trophy for the 1949 and 1950 gunnery meets included an engraved plate naming the four organizations that won the two meets in the two categories.[2]

The story that the trophy was deliberately hidden by racists to cover up the achievement of the black pilots does not ring true. For one thing, the 332d Fighter Group was only one of four organizations listed on the trophy, and three of them were white. Hiding the trophy would not only obscure black heroes, but white ones as well. Another factor to consider is that when the trophy was awarded for the last time, no institution called the Air Force Museum existed yet. In 1956, the Air Force Technical Museum at Wright-Patterson Air Force Base was renamed the Air Force Museum, which was open to the public, but the trophy was not yet a part of the museum's collection and belonged to the Smithsonian Institution, which could not display all of the thousands of artifacts in its inventory. In 1971, the Air Force Museum moved to its current site, but was still only a fraction of what it is today. Not until 1975 was the museum constituted as an official USAF organization rather than simply a named activity. The museum grew tremendously in size in the decades after 1975, and eventually had more room to exhibit artifacts. In 1979, the National Air and Space Museum, a component of the Smithsonian Institution in Washington, transferred some artifacts from the Secretary of the Air Force to the Air Force Museum. Among them was the trophy from the USAF gunnery meets in Las Vegas in 1949 and 1950.[3] Years later, largely through the efforts of Zellie Orr, the trophy for the Air Force's gunnery meets in Las Vegas in 1949 and 1950 was put on display as part of an exhibit to commemorate the achievements of the Tuskegee Airmen, since the 332d Fighter Group was its most famous organization, although the 332d Fighter Group was one of four USAF organizations to win the trophy.[4]

The gunnery meets at Las Vegas were discontinued not because a black group had won, but because the Korean War broke out in 1950, and the Air Force needed to deploy its best fighter groups to the Far East to take part in the conflict, which did not end until 1953.

Every legend has some fact behind it. There was a missing trophy. At the time the large trophy recognizing winners of the 1949 USAF gunnery meet was awarded, smaller trophies, miniature replicas of the large one, were given to the winners in the different divisions. The 332d Fighter Group received a small trophy recognizing its victory in the conventional aircraft division. A photograph taken in 1949 shows both the large and the small trophies. The large trophy is on display at the National Museum of the United States Air Force, but the location of the smaller trophy is unknown.[5]

17

The misconception that the outstanding World War II record of the Tuskegee Airmen alone convinced President Truman to desegregate the armed forces of the United States

The Tuskegee Airmen's 332d Fighter Group completed its combat missions in Europe, and members of the 477th Bombardment Group took part in the "Freeman Field Mutiny," in the spring of 1945, but President Truman did not announce his famous Executive Order 9981 (EO 9981) until July 26, 1948, more than three years later. Although the executive order did not mention segregation or desegregation or integration, President Truman noted that his intent was to end segregation in American military forces, which would help fulfill the equal opportunity the executive order overtly promised.

According to a chronology on the website of the Harry S. Truman Library and Museum, there were several factors that led up to EO 9981. On October 29, 1947, the president's Committee on Civil Rights issued a report, "To Secure These Rights," which called for an end to racial segregation in the armed forces of the United States. On March 27, 1948, twenty African American organizations meeting in New York issued a "Declaration of Negro Voters," which called for an end to racial segregation in the armed forces. On April 26, 1948, sixteen African American leaders told Secretary of Defense James V. Forrestal that the armed forces of the United States must be desegregated. On June 26, 1948, A. Philip Randolph announced the formation of a "League for Non-Violent Civil Disobedience Against Military Segregation," and three days later he told President Truman that unless he issued an executive order ending racial segregation in the armed forces, African American youth would resist the draft.[1] Most importantly, 1948 was a presidential election year, and President Truman hoped to appeal to black voters in his reelection campaign.

All of these factors must have influenced Truman's decision, but I believe the record of the Tuskegee Airmen and the many other black military organizations in World War II, such as the 92d Infantry Division in Italy, black troops who volunteered for front line duty after the Battle of the Bulge, and the black drivers of the "Red Ball Express," must have also been a factor, not only in Truman's mind, but also in the minds of those who urged him to desegregate the military. In recognizing the achievements of black military personnel in World War II, we should not give all the credit to just one or two of those organizations. The Tuskegee Airmen were probably the most famous of the black military organizations in World War II, but they alone were not responsible for the desegregation of the armed forces of the United States.

I believe the exemplary record of the Tuskegee Airmen's 332d Fighter Group during World War II contributed to President Truman's decision to desegregate the United States armed forces, since it proved that black men could fly in combat as well as white men. I believe the efforts of members of the 477th Bombardment Group to desegregate facilities at Freeman Field in 1945 also contributed to the end of racial segregation on military bases, and, ultimately, to the end of racial segregation in the armed forces. However, there were certainly other factors that contributed to President Truman's military desegregation decision, including the role of other black military organizations during World War II.

Another factor to consider is that the Air Force, as a newly independent service, was already moving toward racial integration even before Truman's Executive Order 9981 and that the Air Force actually contributed to the decision. The first secretary of the Air Force, Stuart Symington, supported the racial integration of the Air Force from the beginning of its existence as a military service independent from the Army in 1947, and he contributed to the drafting of the executive order. Symington was an old friend of Truman, and they both hailed from Missouri. Col. Noel Parrish, who had commanded the flying school at Tuskegee Army Air Field, also supported the racial integration of the Air Force before the actual integration was implemented in 1949. It should not be a surprise that the Air Force, of all the military services, was the first one to implement racial integration, because the ball had been rolling within the Air Force even before Truman issued his mandate to all the services.[2]

In a letter dated April 5, 1948, to Lemuel E. Graves of the *Pittsburgh Courier*, General Carl Spaatz, chief of staff of the United States Air Force, wrote, "It is the feeling of this Headquarters that the ultimate Air Force objective must be to eliminate segregation among its personnel by the unrestricted use of Negro personnel in free competition for any duty within the Air Force for which they may qualify." On April 26, Spaatz announced that the Air Force would integrate. His views were consistent with those of the then Secretary of the Air Force, Stuart Symington. Supporting the same view was Lt. Gen. Idwal H. Edwards, Air Force deputy chief of staff for personnel, who thought that racial segregation of the Air Force degraded its effectiveness as a service. In the same month, April 1948, Assistant Secretary of the Air Force Eugene Zuckert testified before the National Defense Conference on Negroes Affairs that the "Air Force accepts no doctrine of racial superiority or inferiority." Lt. Gen. Edwards also testified before the same conference, but was more specific, endorsing desegregation of the Air Force. The United States Air Force had not integrated before Truman's Executive Order 9981, but its leadership had already expressed its desire for racial integration. In the back of the minds of all the Air Force leaders who supported the racial integration of their service before Truman's order, there must have been an awareness of what the only American black pilots in combat in World War II had achieved just a few years earlier, as members of the Army Air Forces.[3]

According to Alan Gropman's book *The Air Force Integrates*, Lt. Gen. Idwal H. Edwards, Air Force deputy chief of staff for personnel, thought racial segregation in the Air Force should end not because the "Negro flying units" of World War II had been effective, but because they had NOT been effective. As a member of the McCloy Committee during the war, he was in a position to know.

This is opposite to the general claim that the segregated units had performed so well they caused segregation to end. There is some logic to that. If the segregated units performed better, people might have argued that segregated units should be maintained.

Col. Noel Parrish, in his Air Command and Staff School thesis in 1947, makes a similar point, noting that "each establishment of a 'Negro unit' project was finally covered with a smoke screen of praise which clouded the issues and obscured the facts." In other words, praising the all-black units too much did not further the cause of integration but segregation. Parrish wanted segregated units to end. The fact that segregation was inefficient proved the need for integration instead.

18

The misconception that 332d Fighter Group was the only group to paint the tails of its fighters a distinctive color, to distinguish them from the fighters of the other fighter escort groups

A popular story about the Tuskegee Airmen is that one day someone in the 332d Fighter Group impulsively decided to paint the tails of the group's escort fighters red so that others would "know who they were" and so that they would get credit for being the best of the fighter escort groups in the combat theater. The story suggests that aircraft of the other fighter escort groups were not painted in any distinctive color, and that the Tuskegee Airmen were the only ones to fly fighters with red tails.[1]

In truth, each of the seven fighter escort groups in the Fifteenth Air Force had its own assigned color marking scheme. By the middle of July 1944, the 306th Fighter Wing had four P-51 groups, of which the 332d Fighter Group was one, and three P-38s groups. The prescribed aircraft markings involved not only the tail but other parts of the aircraft as well, but the tails of the P-51s were the most distinctive. The 31st Fighter Group had striped red-tailed P-51s, while the 52d Fighter Group had yellow-tailed Mustangs. The tails of the 325th Fighter Group P-51s were painted a black and yellow checkerboard pattern, and the 332d Fighter Group, of course, had solid red tails. A Fifteenth Air Force document from 1944 shows the markings of the aircraft of each of the seven fighter groups, and a description of the markings. James T. Sheppard, a Tuskegee Airmen who maintained P-47 and P-51 aircraft at Ramitelli Air Field in Italy when the 332d Fighter Group was flying combat missions from there, remembered that the 332d Fighter Group members did not spontaneously determine the red-tailed markings of their aircraft, but that they were assigned by order of the commander of the Fifteenth Air Force, Gen. Nathan B. Twining. Having received the color scheme order, the maintenance officer of each of the four fighter squadrons of the 332d Fighter Group gathered his crew chiefs and passed along the prescribed aircraft markings.[2]

Once each of the fighter escort group aircraft was painted as assigned, each group could be identified more easily not only by the other fighter groups but also by the bombardment groups and wings whom they would escort. The colors helped the members of the large formations tell friend from foe, and, among friends, which group was which. This was especially important when there were several different bombardment groups and fighter escort groups on the same mission.

19

The misconception that all black military pilot training during World War II took place at Tuskegee Institute

Many articles about the Tuskegee Airmen imply or insinuate that all the black pilots in the American military during World War II received their flight training at Tuskegee Institute.[1] However, there were three main phases of military flight training: primary, basic, and advanced. Only the primary phase took place at Tuskegee Institute.

Along with other black institutions of higher learning, Tuskegee Institute operated a civilian pilot training program at Kennedy Field, south of downtown Tuskegee. This program, however, was to train civilian pilots, who were not yet members of the Army Air Corps or the Army Air Forces. There were other places all over the country where black pilots trained as civilians.

Tuskegee Institute also operated, under contract with the Army Air Forces, a primary flight-training school at Moton Field, another facility owned by Tuskegee Institute. The primary phase was for military pilots, but although the cadets were in the military, many of the instructors were civilians. Military officers supervised the overall training at Moton Field and determined which of the pilots would move on to the basic and advanced phases of military pilot training.

The basic and advanced phases of military pilot training for the Tuskegee Airmen took place not at Tuskegee Institute or any of its facilities, but at Tuskegee Army Air Field, which was several miles northwest of Moton Field. Tuskegee Army Air Field was much larger than Moton Field and was wholly owned and operated by the Army Air Forces. The flying school at Tuskegee Army Air Field was not part of Tuskegee Institute.[2]

20

The misconception that the Tuskegee Airmen were the only fighter pilots following the official policy of "sticking with the bombers"

When Lt. Gen. Ira Eaker commanded the Eighth Air Force in England, his policy for the fighter escorts of his bombers was to "stick with the bombers." That policy was reflected in a sign in the office of the commander of the VIII Fighter Command, Maj. Gen. William Kepner. The sign read: "The first duty of the Eighth Air Force fighters is to bring the bombers back alive."[1] Eaker did not invent the policy that fighter pilots escorting bombers would stay with the bombers and not leave them unprotected by going off chasing after enemy fighters. The policy was already defined in Army Air Forces Field Manual 1–15, "Tactics and Technique of Air Fighting," published on April 10, 1942.[2] It directed fighter escort pilots to "carry out their defensive role."

The policy apparently applied not only to the Eighth Air Force in England, but also to the Fifteenth Air Force in Italy. At the beginning of 1944, Lt. Gen. Eaker moved from England to the Mediterranean Theater of Operations, and became commander of the Mediterranean Allied Air Forces, under which the Fifteenth Air Force operated. In his autobiography, Col. Benjamin O. Davis Jr. mentioned that Lt. Gen. Eaker requested the 332d Fighter Group be given the bomber escort mission and move to join the Fifteenth Air Force. In the same book, Davis insisted that the mission of his fighters was to "stick with the bombers" in order to prevent them from being shot down.[3] From these sources, it appears that the policy of "sticking with the bombers" prevailed at the time the 332d Fighter Group assumed and performed its bomber escort missions. One would therefore assume that if other fighter groups did not "stick with the bombers," but abandoned them to chase after enemy aircraft, that those other fighter groups were not following the policy they were assigned.

There is evidence that by the beginning of 1944, six months before the 332d Fighter Group began escorting bombers of the Fifteenth Air Force, that the official policy had changed. As early as November 1943, Gen. Henry "Hap" Arnold, commander of the Army Air Forces, sent a memorandum to Gen. George C. Marshall, the Army chief of staff, recommending that his fighters "seek out and destroy the German Air Force in the air and on the ground" and that "the defensive concept of our fighter commands and air defense units must be changed to the offensive."[4] In a Christmas 1943 letter to Maj. Gen James H. Doolittle, then commander of the Fifteenth Air Force in Italy, Gen. Arnold wrote "my personal message to you——this is a MUST—is to destroy the enemy air force wherever you find them, in the air, on the ground, and in the factories."[5] In January, 1944, Doolittle moved to England to take command of the Eighth Air Force. Meeting with the commander of the VIII Fighter Command, Maj. Gen. William Kepner, Doolittle told Kepner to take the sign down that said the first duty of the Eighth Air Force fighters was to bring the bombers back alive and to replace it with another sign stating that the first duty of the Eighth Air Force was to destroy enemy aircraft.[6]

One might imagine that Doolittle changed the fighter escort policy of the Eighth Air Force in England, and that the old policy of "sticking with the bombers" was preserved in other theaters, but there is evidence that the policy also changed for the Fifteenth Air Force in Italy. Although the Fifteenth Air Force was technically under the Mediterranean Allied Air Forces, which Eaker commanded, it was also under the operational control, like the Eighth Air Force, of the U.S. Strategic Air Forces in Europe, under the command of Gen. Carl Spaatz. Spaatz, who was the superior of both Doolittle and Eaker, issued an operational directive on January 11, 1944, that directed attacks on the German Air Force in the air and on the ground. Like his superior, Gen. Arnold, Spaatz favored that the fighters go after the enemy aircraft. Even if Eaker desired to preserve the former policy of sticking with the bombers, his superiors directed that the fighters be turned loose against the German fighters as early as the end of 1943 and January 1944. This new policy was more practical in light of the increasing numbers and range of the Allied fighter escorts. Some of the fighters could be spared to go after the enemy aircraft, shooting them down so they could never threaten the bombers again. The 332d Fighter Group did not begin escorting heavy bombers of the Fifteenth Air Force until June 1944, about six months after the policy began to change. Even when the 332d Fighter Group did begin escorting heavy bombers, there were times when the group's own escort fighters were allowed to go in search of enemy fighters and airfields.

According to Richard Davis's biography of Spaatz, *Carl A. Spaatz and the Air War in Europe,* "Spaatz contributed greatly to the defeat of the Luftwaffe. He put his whole authority behind the decision to employ aggressive, loose-escort tactics, which freed the fighters to seek out the enemy but left the bombers more vulnerable." As commander of the U.S. Strategic Air Forces in

Europe, by the end of February 1944 (at least three months before the 332d Fighter Group began flying bomber escort missions), Gen. Spaatz provided operational control to both the Eighth Air Force in England under Doolittle, and the Fifteenth Air Force in Italy under Twining.[7]

In conclusion, if the fighter escort groups of the Fifteenth Air Force, besides the 332d Fighter Group, sometimes chased after enemy aircraft instead of only "sticking with the bombers," it appears that they were following rather than violating policy, and that the new policy emanated not from them but from the highest officers of the Army Air Forces. Contrary to a common misconception, the other fighter pilots were not simply seeking to raise their aerial victory credits total for personal glory and abandoning the bombers they were supposed to protect in violation of their assigned mission.

21

The misconception that the Tuskegee Airmen's 332d Fighter Group flew more different kinds of aircraft in combat than any other Army Air Forces group during World War II

I am not certain how this misconception originated, but it appeared at the Enlisted Heritage Hall, a museum at Gunter Annex of Maxwell Air Force Base. A display plaque claimed that the 332d Fighter Group, the only Tuskegee Airmen group in combat, flew more different kinds of aircraft in combat in World War II than any other group in the Army Air Forces.[1]

The 332d Fighter Group flew a total of four different kinds of aircraft during World War II: P-39s, P-40s, P-47s, and P-51s.[2] There were other Army Air Forces groups that flew four or more aircraft in combat during the war. One of them was the 8th Fighter Group, that flew P-38s, P-39s, P-40s, and P-47s, according to the lineage and honors histories of the component squadrons. The 8th Fighter Group also flew P-400s, but that was another version of the P-39. It appears from this research that the 8th Fighter Group, like the 332d Fighter Group, also flew four different kinds of aircraft in combat during World War II.[3]

Research by Barry Spink of the Air Force Historical Research Agency indicates that the 1st Air Commando Group flew more than four kinds of aircraft during World War II and might have flown as many as nine different types: B-25 bombers, P-51 fighters, L-1 and L-5 liaison airplanes, C-47 transports, CG-4 and TG-5 gliders, UC-64 utility airplanes, and even helicopters. It appears from preliminary research that it was the 1st Air Commando Group, not the 332d Fighter Group of the Tuskegee Airmen, that flew more different kinds of aircraft in combat than any other Army Air Forces group during World War II.[4]

22

The misconception that the Tuskegee Airmen belonged to some of the most highly decorated units in U.S. military history

In various places, one finds articles that claim the Tuskegee Airmen belonged to units that were among the most highly decorated in U.S. history. For example, an article by Jessica York titled "Tuskegee Airmen Recall Flying Unfriendly Skies," published in the *Oroville (Calif.) Mercury Register* on February 20, 2007, claimed about the Tuskegee Airmen, "To their great credit, many units rose far above the expectations of their often racist commanders- some becoming among the most highly decorated units in U.S. military history." A similar claim appears in a 2013 online advertisement for the book *The Tuskegee Airmen and Beyond* by David G. Styles. It mentions that the Tuskegee Airmen belonged to one of the most highly decorated of the Army Air Forces organizations in World War II, at least in their theater.

The first black flying squadron in the American military was the 99th Fighter Squadron, but it was far from the most highly decorated of the fighter squadrons in the Air Force during World War II. The 99th Fighter Squadron earned a service streamer, twelve campaign streamers, and three Distinguished Unit Citations during the war. The 94th Fighter Squadron, which was not a Tuskegee Airmen unit, earned sixteen campaign streamers and three Distinguished Unit Citations during World War II. Even in its theater, the 99th Fighter Squadron was not the most highly decorated. The 309th Fighter Squadron, an example of a non-Tuskegee Airmen unit that was based in the same theater during World War II, earned a total of fifteen campaign streamers, two with arrowheads, as well as two Distinguished Unit Citations. There were other fighter squadrons in the theater, without Tuskegee Airmen members, that had comparable numbers of honors.[1]

The Tuskegee Airmen's 332d Fighter Group, the only black flying group in combat during World War II, received ten campaign streamers and one Distinguished Unit Citation during World War II. The 1st Fighter Group, which was not a Tuskegee Airmen group, received fifteen campaign streamers during the war, and three Distinguished Unit Citations. Even in comparison to other fighter groups in the same numbered air force and the same theater during

World War II, the 332d Fighter Group was hardly the most decorated. The white 31st Fighter Group, which also flew in the same combat theater during World War II, received fifteen campaign streamers and two Distinguished Unit Citations. There were other fighter groups in the same theater that also earned comparable honors to the 31st.[2]

If the 99th Fighter Squadron and the 332d Fighter Group suffered from racial discrimination by their commanders during World War II, how could they have expected to have been among the most highly decorated organizations in the Army Air Forces? If they had been among the most highly decorated organizations, the claim of racism against them, by higher commanders, would be difficult to defend.

Individual pilots also earned awards, such as Distinguished Flying Crosses and Air Medals, during World War II, but the Tuskegee Airmen did not earn more individual awards than those who were members of other groups and squadrons in the same theater.

The idea that the Tuskegee Airmen were more highly decorated than the pilots of any other flying unit, even in their theater during World War II, is not supported by the evidence. The honors of the groups and squadrons show that the Tuskegee Airmen organizations, in fact, were less highly decorated than some of the other Army Air Forces flying organizations with which they served during World War II.

23

The misconception that the Tuskegee Airmen never got the recognition they deserved

One often reads or hears that the Tuskegee Airmen never got the recognition they deserved.[1] The claim was true at first, when in the first couple of decades after World War II, most of the unit histories remained classified and general histories of the war and the role of the Army Air Forces in the war tended to ignore the black units and not mention the Tuskegee Airmen at all. But the claim is no longer true, and at times the 332d Fighter Group and the 99th Fighter Squadron receive more publicity than many of the other squadrons and groups that served with them in the Twelfth and Fifteenth Air Forces.

As early as 1955, Charles Francis published a book about the black flying units in World War II titled *The Tuskegee Airmen: The Men Who Changed a Nation*. In fact, Francis coined the term Tuskegee Airmen. Whoever read the book became aware that there were black pilots in combat with the American armed forces during World War II, but the book was not widely known at first.[2]

A second event that further publicized the role of the black airmen in World War II was the formation of the Tuskegee Airmen Incorporated. Tuskegee Airmen veterans began gathering in 1972, and in 1975, they incorporated. In 1978, the leaders of the organization amended the articles of incorporation to make the Tuskegee Airmen Incorporated a charitable and educational organization. The Tuskegee Airmen Incorporated has ever since educated the public about the contributions of the Tuskegee Airmen in World War II.[3]

A third event made the Tuskegee Airmen famous around the nation and around the world. In 1995, the HBO cable television station produced and showed a movie called *The Tuskegee Airmen*, starring Lawrence Fishburne and Cuba Gooding Jr. The movie was very popular, and not long after its premiere, "Tuskegee Airmen" became a common term. More and more Americans were aware of the black pilots who served in the Army Air Forces during World War II. In 1998, President Bill Clinton pinned a fourth star on the uniform of the most famous of the Tuskegee Airmen officers, Gen. Benjamin O. Davis Jr., who had already become the first black general in the U.S. Air Force. By then, Gen. Daniel "Chappie" James, another Tuskegee Airman, had become the first black four-star general in any of the armed forces of the United States.[4] By this time, the Tuskegee Airmen were becoming more famous than many of the white airmen who served in other organizations flying some of the same kinds of missions in the same theater.

A fourth event made the Tuskegee Airmen even more famous nationwide. In March 2007, in an impressive ceremony in the rotunda of the U.S. Capitol in Washington, D.C., President George W. Bush awarded the Congressional Gold Medal to the Tuskegee Airmen. The event was televised nationally. The Congressional Gold Medal is the highest civilian honor awarded by Congress, and it was presented to honor the Tuskegee Airmen collectively. Surviving Tuskegee Airmen from around the nation gathered for the ceremony. President Bush himself saluted the Tuskegee Airmen for their World War II service and apologized, on behalf of the United States, for the mistreatment they suffered in the past.

A fifth event that further publicized the Tuskegee Airmen nationally and around the world was the 2012 release of the film *Red Tails*, which George Lucas produced. While the movie had mixed reviews, it was widely popular. George Lucas, who was world famous for his *Star Wars* and *Indiana Jones* movie series, helped spread the fame of the Tuskegee Airmen far and wide, and the Tuskegee Airmen Incorporated, at their 2012 national convention in Las Vegas, recognized Lucas in an impressive ceremony.

In addition to the Tuskegee Airmen book by Charles Francis, the formation of the Tuskegee Airmen Incorporated, the 2007 Congressional Gold Medal Ceremony, and the release of the *Red Tails* and *The Tuskegee Airmen* movies, the Tuskegee Airmen became famous in many other ways. They have been honored in countless other books, magazines, and newspaper articles. Their story has also been celebrated in special museum exhibits, including the National Museum of the United States Air Force, the National Air and Space Museum, and the National World War II Museum. There is a Tuskegee Airmen National Historic Site at Tuskegee, run by the National Park Service of the Department of the Interior. There are even air shows in which a Red Tail Squadron of the Commemorative Air Force flies a red-tailed P-51. For all of these reasons, the claim that the Tuskegee Airmen never got the recognition they deserved is no longer true. People might not have heard about the Tuskegee Airmen for many years after World War II, but by the turn of the twenty-first century, they were among the most famous of the World War II pilots of the Army Air Forces. In fact, the Tuskegee Airmen were more famous than the members of many of the white flying organizations with whom they served in the Twelfth and Fifteenth Air Forces during World War II. They became so famous that some persons came to think of them as the only fighter escorts in their theater of operations, when in reality they were one of seven fighter escort groups in the Fifteenth Air Force.

Sometimes one hears or reads the claim that the Tuskegee Airmen were "excluded from World War II victory parades." The implication is that all the returning veterans had victory parades and that the organizers of victory parades in various places deliberately excluded the black pilots. There were a great many returning veterans during the war who never got a victory parade, and not all of them were black. There are also photographs of black servicemembers in parades just after World War II, and they were certainly celebrated in African American communities and in newspapers such as the *Chicago Defender* and the *Pittsburgh Courier*. In fact, during the war, the black press was filled with stories celebrating what the black pilots were doing and what they had done. They certainly were not ignored everywhere.

24

The misconception that Tuskegee Airman Charles McGee flew more combat missions than any other pilot in the Air Force, or more combat missions than any other Air Force fighter pilot, or more combat missions than any other USAF pilot in three wars

Sometimes one hears or reads the claim that Tuskegee Airman Col. Charles McGee, who flew combat missions as a fighter pilot not only in World War II but also in Korea, and Vietnam, compiled a record of more combat missions than any other Air Force pilot. The claim appeared in an old edition of *Rising Above*, a booklet published by the Commemorative Air Force's Red Tail Squadron to celebrate the achievements of the Tuskegee Airmen. That edition, circulating in 2012, claimed that Col. McGee and his 409 combat missions hold the U.S. Air Force record for most combat missions ever flown.[1] In reality, there were many other Air Force pilots with more combat missions than Col. McGee.

The source of the claim was not Col. McGee himself or the Tuskegee Airmen. A version of the claim was contained in a 1994 speech by former Air Force Chief of Staff Gen. Ronald Fogleman at the Tuskegee Airmen Incorporated national convention in Atlanta, Georgia. Gen. Fogleman noted that Col. McGee had the distinction of having flown more fighter missions than any other pilot in the three-war history of the Air Force. Gen. Fogleman's words are contained in a biography of Col. McGee by his daughter, Dr. Charlene McGee Smith. The same source notes that Charles McGee flew 409 combat missions. If you read the book carefully, you realize that the claim of more combat missions than any other Air Force pilot might be a misinterpretation of Gen. Fogleman's meaning. He might have meant not that Col. McGee compiled more combat missions than any other USAF pilot but more than any other USAF fighter pilot who also served in three wars.[2] Even then, the claim is not accurate.

There were several U.S. Air Force pilots who flew more than 409 combat missions and therefore more than Col. McGee. Aldophus H. "Pat" Bledsoe Jr., in an email to the marketing director of the CAF Red Tail Squadron, noted that he had flown 422 combat missions in Vietnam and was aware of several other Air Force pilots who flew more than 500 missions during that war. However, Bledsoe was a forward air controller (FAC) and not a fighter pilot, and he referred to other USAF pilots who were FACs and not fighter pilots. Col. Alan Gropman flew 671 missions in Vietnam, a total much higher than McGee's 409, but Gropman flew transports, not fighters.[3] Lloyd J. Probst, another USAF transport pilot, is reported to have flown 1,248 combat missions during the Vietnam War.[4] Probst flew C-130s. Col. McGee definitely did not fly more combat missions than any other USAF pilot.

TABLE 13 · USAF Pilots Known to Have Flown at Least Four Hundred Combat Missions.

Name	World War II	Korea	Southeast Asia	Total
Lloyd J. Probst (transport pilot)			1,248	1,248
Philip Anderson (transport pilot)			1,000+	1,000+
Jay Soukup (transport pilot)			935	935
James P. Fleming			810 (helicopter)	810
Alan Gropman (transport pilot)			671	671
Harold S. Snow (fighter and FAC pilot)	100	101	465 missions (130 of these were fighter combat missions)	666 (331 of these were fighter combat missions)
Ralph S. Parr (fighter pilot)	12	202	427	641
Don Kilgus (fighter pilot)			624	624
Kenneth R. Hughey (fighter pilot)			564	564
Donald Blakeslee	Nearly 500			Nearly 500
Major James Cronk (fighter pilot)			480	480
Adolphus H. "Pat" Bledsoe (FAC pilot)			422	422
Charles E. McGee (fighter pilot)	136	100	173	409

Sources: For Anderson: Gerry May, "Hometown Patriot," KTBS, https://www.ktbs.com/phil-anderson-flew-more-than-a-thousand-combat-missions-in-vietnam-war/video_3f89d867-do4c-53d1-a737-ac8080d26d48.html. For Soukup: Abby Weingarten, "Pilot Flew 935 Missions in Vietnam," Herald Tribune, September 3, 2015, https://www.heraldtribune.com/story/news/2015/09/03/pilot-flew-935-missions-in-vietnam/29324918007. For Fleming: Major Donald K. Schneider, Air Force Heroes in Vietnam (Washington, D.C.: U.S. Government Printing Office, 1979), 35. For Snow: John Mollison, 666, the Devil's Number: The Amazing Service of Hank Snow (2013), JohnMollison.com; and Terry Brown, "Fighter Pilot Who Flew 666 Combat Missions in Three Wars Dies," Times Union, https://www.timesunion.com/tuplus-local/article/Figher-pilot-who-flew-666-combat-missions-in-10616779.php. For Parr: Air Force Magazine, February 1987, 109; Daedalus Flyer, Summer 1996, 15–21. For Blakeslee: article by Dennis Hevisi, "Col. Donald Blakeslee, Decorated World War II Flying Ace, Dies at 90," New York Times, October 3, 2008. For McGee: Charlene E. McGee Smith, Tuskegee Airman: The Biography of Charles E. McGee (Boston: Branden Publishing Company, 1999).

Note: There may be other USAF pilots who flew more than 409 combat missions.

If McGee did not fly more combat missions than any other Air Force pilot, did he fly more combat missions than any other Air Force fighter pilot? There were other Air Force pilots who flew fighters and who also flew more than 409 combat missions. One of them was Maj. Kenneth Raymond Hughey, who flew 564 combat missions in Vietnam before he was shot down and became a prisoner of war. His number of combat fighter missions is 155 more than the 409 combat missions of Col. McGee, but unlike McGee, he did not fly in three wars.[5] Maj. James Cronk was another USAF fighter pilot who flew more combat missions than Col. McGee. Cronk flew 480 combat missions in Vietnam, flying F-4 fighters, but he did not fly in three wars.[6] Don Kilgus, a fighter pilot whom his brother claims had eight tours of duty in Vietnam between 1964 and 1973, is reputed to have flown 624 fighter combat missions in that war.[7]

If Col. McGee did not fly more combat missions than any other USAF pilot, and if he did not fly more combat missions than any other USAF fighter pilot, did he fly more combat missions than any other Air Force fighter pilot who flew in three wars? That claim would also be false. At least two other Air Force fighter pilots who flew in World War II, Korea, and Vietnam flew more combat missions than Col. McGee. One of them was Col. Ralph S. Parr. His total number of fighter combat missions in the three wars is 641. He flew 12 missions in P-38s during World War II, 165 missions in F-80s and 37 missions in F-86s during the Korean War, and 427 missions in F-4s during two tours of duty in the Vietnam War.[8] Col. Harold S. Snow was another Air Force pilot who also flew fighters in World War II, Korea, and Vietnam. His total number of combat missions is 666. He flew 100 missions during World War II, 101 missions during the Korean War, and 465 additional missions in Southeast Asia.[9] Some say that McGee was the only pilot with at least one hundred combat missions as a fighter pilot in three wars, but Snow was also a fighter pilot in the same three wars and flew at least one hundred combat missions in all three of them. However, most of Snow's combat missions in Vietnam were not fighter missions.

Col. McGee appears to have been one of two USAF pilots to have flown at least one hundred fighter combat missions in each of three wars: World War II, Korea, and Vietnam. McGee flew 136 in World War II, 100 in Korea, and 173 in Vietnam, while Snow flew 100 in World War II, 101 in Korea, and 130 in Vietnam. If one adds up their fighter combat missions in the three wars, McGee has the higher total, 409 compared with Snow's 331. However, if one adds Snow's 335 liaison/forward air control combat missions in Vietnam, Snow has more combat missions than McGee in the three wars.

Col. Charles McGee should be honored for having flown 409 combat missions as a fighter pilot in the Air Force and for having flown in three wars, World War II, Korea, and Vietnam, but the claim that he flew more combat missions than any other USAF pilot, more combat missions than any other USAF fighter pilot, or more combat missions than any other USAF fighter pilot in three wars, is false.

25

The misconception that all U.S. black military pilots during World War II were Tuskegee Airmen in the Army Air Forces

Not all black military pilots who served in the U.S. military during World War II were Tuskegee Airmen and not all of them belonged to the Army Air Forces. Before August 1943, nine black military pilots in the U.S. Army graduated from advanced liaison pilot training at Fort Sill, Oklahoma, instead of at Tuskegee. Six of these individuals had "washed out" of previous flight training at Tuskegee Army Air Field before transferring to Fort Sill. In other words, they did not earn their pilot wings at Tuskegee but at Fort Sill. Three other black liaison pilots trained with future white liaison pilots at Denton, Texas, and Pittsburg, Kansas, before they moved on to advanced liaison flight training and graduation at Fort Sill. Those nine were not technically Tuskegee Airmen pilots and not members of the Army Air Forces when they earned their pilot wings, although they were most definitely among black military pilots who served in the U.S. military during World War II. However, compared to the total number of black pilots, they were very few. There were 992 black military pilots in the U.S. military during World War II who were Tuskegee Airmen because they graduated from advanced pilot training at Tuskegee Army Air Field. Among them were fifty-one liaison pilots.[1]

26

The misconception that Daniel "Chappie" James, the first four-star black general in the U.S. military services, was among the leaders of the "Freeman Field Mutiny" in April 1945

In his biography of Gen. Daniel "Chappie" James Jr., *Black Eagle: General Daniel 'Chappie' James, Jr.*, James R. McGovern repeated a story that Gen. James was involved in the Freeman Field Mutiny as one of its leaders who refused to sign a document to acknowledge segregated officers' clubs at Freeman Field and who was arrested for that refusal. The book suggests that despite James's earlier defiance of an order, he rose to the highest rank in the U.S. Air Force: four-star general.[1]

Daniel "Chappie" James belonged to the 477th Bombardment Group at Freeman Field at the time of the "mutiny" there, but he was not one of the sixty-one black officers who were arrested on April 5 and 6, 1945, for attempting to enter the officers' club reserved for whites. All but three of those officers were quickly released. James was also not one of the 101 black officers who were arrested later for refusing to obey an order to sign a paper acknowledging the two separate officers' clubs at Freeman Field, when they were given that chance on April 9–11, 1945. Le Roy F. Gillead, who was among those arrested both times, listed all the officers who were arrested in both cases. Historian Dr. Alan Gropman, who interviewed Gen. James, and historian Guy Franklin, who studied the issue and found orders listing the arrested officers, confirmed that James was not one of the arrested officers. Maj. John D. Murphy, an Air Command and Staff College student at Air University, wrote a paper called "The Freeman Field Mutiny: A Study in Leadership" in 1997. In two appendixes, Maj. Murphy listed all the black officers who were arrested in the Freeman Field Mutiny, and Daniel James was not on either list. The second appendix, which includes the names of the 101 officers arrested for refusing to sign a document recognizing the policy of segregated officers' clubs, is Freeman Field Special Order 87 dated April 12, 1945. I must conclude that then Lt. Daniel "Chappie" James either obeyed the order to sign the document acknowledging segregated officers' clubs at Freeman Field, or he was absent from the base at the time. He was not one of the leaders of the Freeman Field Mutiny.[2]

At the time of the Freeman Field Mutiny, in April 1945, there were 422 black officers there. Only 101 refused to sign the base regulation specifying separate officers' clubs. If Lt. Daniel "Chappie" James was not among the 101 and signed the regulation, he must have been among the 76 percent of black officers there who did not join the Freeman Field mutiny. If he was not among the participants of the mutiny, then he could not have been among its leaders.[3]

27

The misconception that the Tuskegee Airmen's 332d Fighter Group flew more combat missions than any other unit in Europe during World War II

In the book *American Patriots: The Story of Blacks in the Military from the Revolution to Desert Storm*, Gail Buckley twice repeated another misconception regarding the Tuskegee Airmen: "the 332d flew more missions than any other unit in Europe," 1,578 combat missions in all.[1] Gail Buckley is the daughter of Lena Horne, the famous black singer and actress who knew many of the Tuskegee Airmen.

The 332d Fighter Group did not fly more combat missions than any other unit in Europe. The 1,578 combat missions number includes 578 missions of the 99th Fighter Squadron before July 1944, when it moved to the 332d Fighter Group base and began flying missions as one of its assigned squadrons.[2] Before that, the 99th Fighter Squadron had been attached to other groups. During World War II, the 332d Fighter Group actually flew a total of 914 missions, 602 with the Twelfth Air Force and 312 with the Fifteenth Air Force.[3] The 31st Fighter Group, which also served in Italy during World War II, flew 930 missions during the war.[4] Why did the 31st Fighter Group fly more missions than the 332d Fighter Group? The answer is simple. The 31st Fighter Group entered combat much earlier than the 332d Fighter Group. The 31st Fighter Group had more opportunity to accumulate a higher number of combat missions.[5]

Other fighter groups in Europe flew even more combat missions than the 31st Fighter Group during the war. An example is the 57th Fighter Group, which flew more than sixteen hundred combat missions.[6] The 57th Fighter Group had an advantage over the 31st and 332d Fighter Groups because it did not have to escort heavy bombers. Fighter groups that escorted B-17s and B-24s flew an average of only one or two missions per day, while fighter groups supporting ground forces could fly several missions per day. The 332d Fighter Group flew many more missions per day on average before it began escorting heavy bombers in June 1944.

Sometimes one also reads that the Tuskegee Airmen flew more than fifteen thousand combat missions during World War II, but that is even further from the truth.[7] Whoever claims that figure is looking at combat sorties, which were different from combat missions. Together, the 99th Fighter Squadron (before it was assigned to the 332d Fighter Group) and the 332d Fighter Group flew a total of more than fifteen thousand sorties. If twenty-five fighters of a unit took part in a combat mission, the unit flew twenty-five sorties on that one combat mission. A unit flew as many sorties as it flew aircraft on a given mission. Did the 332d Fighter Group fly more combat sorties than any other unit in Europe during World War II? No. Other fighter groups in Europe flew well over fifteen thousand combat sorties. For example, the 57th Fighter Group flew more than thirty-eight thousand sorties.[8] Why the 57th Fighter Group flew many more sorties than the 332d Fighter Group is very understandable. The 57th Fighter Group entered combat in October 1942, while the 332d Fighter Group entered combat in February 1944. The 57th Fighter Group had a head start of fifteen months.[9]

28

The misconception that Col. Benjamin O. Davis Jr., by ordering his pilots to "stick with the bombers," put his pilots in greater danger than the white pilots and gave them less opportunity to become aces

A Tuskegee Airman named Le Roy F. Gillead, one of the Tuskegee Airmen who was arrested for attempting to desegregate a white officers' club at Freeman Field, published a book about the Tuskegee Airmen in 1994 called *The Tuskegee Aviation Experiment and Tuskegee Airmen 1939–1949: America's Black Air Force for World War II.* In his book, Gillead criticized Col. Benjamin O. Davis Jr. as if he had put the black pilots in the 332d Fighter Group in greater danger and prevented them from becoming aces by ordering them to "stick with the bombers" they were escorting. Gillead called such missions "suicide" and suggested that Davis conspired with white officers to keep the black pilots "in their place" by ordering such missions.[1]

How could Gillead have come to those conclusions? Gillead believed Col. Davis was a "West Point martinet."[2] He must have imagined that when Col. Davis ordered his men to "stick with the bombers" and "not go chasing after enemy airplanes," he wanted his pilots to maneuver their aircraft between the escorted bombers and the enemy aircraft so that the black-occupied fighters rather than the white-occupied bombers would be shot down. He must have thought that close bomber escort did not involve shooting down enemy airplanes but merely getting in their way. If that were the case, the black pilots would not have had the opportunity to shoot down any enemy airplanes or become aces for having shot down at least five of them.

The author was not one of the fighter pilots who actually escorted bombers over Europe during World War II. If he had been, he would have known that the purpose of the fighter escorts flying with the bombers was not merely to get between the enemy fighters and the escorted bombers but to shoot down those enemy aircraft that came close to the bombers. Yes, Davis did not want his fellow black combat pilots to abandon the bombers by chasing enemy aircraft that were sent to lure them far away from the bomber formations, but he certainly did want his pilots to shoot down enemy aircraft if those aircraft were attacking the bombers they were assigned to escort. That is the only way the bombers would really be protected. The bombers in fact attracted enemy fighters, giving the escort fighters a chance to shoot them down. The 332d Fighter Group shot down many more aircraft after its assignment to the Fifteenth Air Force for bomber escort than before. While Davis himself did not shoot down any enemy aircraft, despite flying many missions with his group, his fellow black pilots shot down a host of enemy airplanes on their bomber escort missions. The black aerial victories were not achieved in spite of Davis's orders but because of them. The 332d Fighter Group and its squadrons shot down a total of 112 enemy airplanes, a great many of them during bomber escort missions between early June 1944 and the end of April 1945. There were no black aces, but the reason was less because of Col. Davis's bomber escort policy than because of the fact that most of the 332d Fighter Group missions, after July 1944, encountered no enemy aircraft.[3]

Neither were the bomber escort missions suicidal. In fact, by not chasing enemy aircraft that no longer threatened the escorted bombers, the pilots would have less chance to be shot down by the enemy themselves. The close escort policy protected the bombers but also the fighters that flew with them. Col. Davis's policy gave his black fighter pilots the opportunity to shoot down enemy aircraft without increasing the danger they would face. Instead of restricting the opportunity of the Tuskegee Airmen to survive and gain fame, Davis enhanced it.

29

The misconception that Charles Alfred "Chief" Anderson taught himself how to fly

Charles Alfred "Chief" Anderson is unquestionably one of the most important early black pilots. Often called the "father of black aviation," Anderson was the first black pilot to earn a commercial transport pilot's license, in 1932, and one of the most significant black pilot pioneers because of a 1933 transcontinental flight he made with Dr. Albert E. Forsythe from Atlantic City, New Jersey, to Los Angeles and back. In 1934, he and Forsythe flew through the islands of the Caribbean, and in 1939, Anderson became a civilian pilot instructor at Howard University. In 1940, Anderson became the chief civilian pilot instructor at Tuskegee Institute and eventually became the most important black flight instructor in the primary phase of flight training for the Tuskegee Airmen cadets at Moton Field. Anderson had bought his first airplane in 1929 (a Velie Monocoupe) and with it began to learn how to fly. One of the popular stories about Chief Anderson is that he was forced to teach himself how to fly because no white pilot would teach him.[1]

Chief Anderson did not completely teach himself how to fly. Two white pilots contributed to his flight training. One of them was Russell Thaw, an experienced pilot to whom Anderson lent his airplane for trips between Pennsylvania and Atlantic City, New Jersey, where Thaw's mother lived. Anderson accompanied Thaw on many of those flights, carefully observing him to learn how to fly the aircraft.[2] Anderson also received flight training from Ernst Buehl, a German immigrant who maintained a flight school in the Philadelphia area and had been a transcontinental airmail pilot. Buehl was instrumental in persuading authorities to allow Anderson to take the test for the commercial transport pilot's license because he himself had helped train Anderson how to fly. To say that Chief Anderson taught himself how to fly discounts the contributions of Russell Thaw and Ernst Buehl.[3]

Whether "Chief" Charles Alfred Anderson was the most important flight instructor of the Tuskegee Airmen is debatable. He served in the primary phase of Tuskegee Airmen flight training at Moton Field. However, there were two additional phases, each as long as the first phase: the basic flight-training phase and the advanced flight-training phase. These two subsequent flight-training phases were taught at Tuskegee Army Air Field, several miles to the northwest of Moton Field, where Chief Anderson remained. I have found no evidence that Chief Anderson ever moved from Moton Field to Tuskegee Army Air Field. It is possible that some of the Tuskegee Airmen might have felt that the most important of their flight instructors was not at Moton Field but at Tuskegee Army Air Field, where the second and third phases of their flight training took place in more advanced aircraft.[4]

30

The misconception that Congress passed a law to create the first black flying unit

I attended eight consecutive national conventions of the Tuskegee Airmen Incorporated, and at some of those meetings I heard people claim that Congress created the first black flying unit by law. One published source has phrased the claim this way: "Against the wishes of the War Department, the U.S. Congress, bowing to pressure from Negro leaders and media, activated the first all-black Fighter Squadron at Tuskegee Institute, Alabama."[1]

I have not found any congressional act that created the first all-black flying unit. On April 3, 1939, Congress passed Public Law 76-18, which some interpret as requiring the training of black pilots for the army. The legislation was not specific, however, and did not require the War Department or the air corps to accept black pilots as members. The law only required that the Civil Aeronautics Authority designate a school for the training of black pilots, presumably for future military service.[2]

On September 16, 1940, Congress passed the Burke-Wadsworth Act, which forbade racial restrictions on voluntary enlistments in the branches of the armed forces, including, presumably, the air corps. However, it did not mandate a black flying unit or black pilots.[3] It only required that black Americans be allowed to serve in the air corps. In fact, the air corps began planning to add aviation units that would not fly aircraft but construct airfields instead.[4]

More than a month later, on October 24, the War Department asked the air corps to submit a plan for the establishment and training of a black pursuit squadron. In early December, the air corps submitted such a plan, which called for a black flying unit to be formed, with support personnel to be trained at Chanute Field, Illinois, and with pilots eventually to be trained at Tuskegee. On January 16, 1941, the War Department announced that a black flying unit would be formed within the air corps. In a letter, the War Department constituted the first black flying squadron, the 99th Pursuit Squadron, on March 19, 1941, and activated it the same month at Chanute Field. Thus, it was the War Department, not Congress, that constituted and activated the first black flying unit.[5] Of course, without the pressure of the president, Congress, black political organizations, and the black press, the War Department might never have constituted and activated the first black flying unit.

A threatened lawsuit by Yancey Williams, a black man who sought to be an army pilot, also contributed to the War Department's reluctant decision to allow black pilots in the air corps, if only in a segregated unit. The National Association for the Advancement of Colored People (NAACP) maintained a National Legal Committee, led by Thurgood Marshall, who accepted the case. Around the same time that the Yancey Williams case was filed, the War Department announced that there would be a black flying unit in the air corps and therefore a place for black pilots in the U.S. military.[6]

31

The misconception that black organizations and black newspapers all supported the training of black pilots at Tuskegee

Very general descriptions of the Tuskegee Airmen in history sometimes focus on the idea that pressure from black political organizations and black newspapers forced the War Department to begin training black pilots at Tuskegee and create all-black flying units. One source notes that, "Black pressure, supported by a lawsuit by Howard University student Yancey Williams with the help of the NAACP, finally forced the War Department on January 9, 1941, to authorize the training of black pilots and form the 99th Pursuit Squadron."[1]

Many black leaders, in the National Association for the Advancement of Colored People (NAACP) and in editorial staffs of the leading black newspapers, opposed the segregated training of black pilots at Tuskegee and the creation of all-black flying units because they wanted black pilots to be trained at the same bases as white pilots and for black and white pilots to serve together in racially integrated units. Some of them even called the 99th Fighter Squadron, the first black flying unit, a "Jim Crow air squadron." Judge William Hastie, a black leader who served as a special advisor to the War Department, noted, "I can see no reason whatever for setting up a separate program for Negroes in the Air Corps." Black leaders eventually reluctantly supported the Tuskegee Airmen because having black pilots trained at segregated bases and serving in segregated units was at least better than having no black pilots at all in the Army Air Forces.[2]

32

The misconception that most of the flight instructors of the Tuskegee Airmen were black

"Chief" Charles Alfred Anderson is the most famous of the black flight instructors of the Tuskegee Airmen, and his story sometimes leads people not familiar with the whole story to conclude that Anderson and his fellow black flight instructors at Tuskegee were the majority of the flight instructors who trained the Tuskegee Airmen. A Wikipedia article noted as late as March 18, 2014, that Chief Anderson "was selected by the Army as Tuskegee's Ground Commander and Chief Instructor for aviation cadets of the 99th Pursuit Squadron."[1]

Most of the flight instructors of the Tuskegee Airmen cadets at Moton Field, where the primary phase of flight training took place, were black, but the primary phase was only the first of three flight-training phases, each of equal length. The second and third phases, basic and advanced flight training, took place at Tuskegee Army Air Field, which was located several miles northwest of Moton Field. During most of World War II, all of the flight instructors at Tuskegee Army Air Field, for the basic and advanced flight-training phases, were white. The first black flight-training instructors at Tuskegee Army Air Field did not arrive until the second half of 1944 and most of the flight instructors there continued to be white well into 1945. There were many more white flight instructors at Tuskegee Army Air Field during most of World War II than there were black flight-training instructors at Moton Field because each of the basic and advanced flight-training phases had its own set of instructors. For example, by the end of 1944, Tuskegee Army Air Field had forty-nine flight instructors in the various flying schools (basic, advanced single-engine, advanced twin-engine, fighter transition), but only seven of them were black. Later in the war, increasing numbers of black pilots who had combat experience overseas returned home to become flight instructors at Tuskegee Army Air Field. However, most of the Tuskegee Airmen who deployed overseas during World War II were trained early in the war and their flight instructors in the basic and advanced flight-training phases at Tuskegee Army Air Field were white. As late as the spring of 1945, twenty of the thirty-four basic flight-training instructors at Tuskegee Army Air Field were white. In reality, most of the flight instructors at Tuskegee during World War II were white even though the number of black flying instructors at Tuskegee Army Air Field was growing during the last year of the war.[2]

33

The misconception that Moton Field, location of the Tuskegee Airmen National Historic Site, was Tuskegee Army Air Field, where most black flight training took place during World War II

In a book called *America's Beautiful National Parks*, Aaron J. McKean repeated a common misconception that Moton Field, where the Tuskegee Airmen National Historic Site is today, was the location of Tuskegee Army Air Field.[1] Many visitors who come to the site, like McKean, think that it was where the bulk of the Tuskegee Airmen's flight training occurred during World War II.

Moton Field was actually the place where only the primary flight training took place, using biplanes on grass. The two subsequent flight-training phases, basic and advanced, took place at a much larger airfield several miles to the northwest of Moton Field, with more advanced aircraft types. That was the location of Tuskegee Army Air Field, with extensive paved runways and a great many more facilities. By the middle of the war, each of the three flight-training phases took approximately nine weeks. Two-thirds of the flight training took place at Tuskegee Army Air Field, not Moton Field.[2]

The "Black Wings" exhibit in the National Air and Space Museum made a similar mistake. It displayed a photograph of Eleanor Roosevelt in an airplane with Charles Alfred "Chief" Anderson, a black flying instructor, and incorrectly identified the place as Tuskegee Army Air Field. The photograph was actually taken at the end of March 1941 at Kennedy Field, miles away from both Moton Field and Tuskegee Army Air Field, both of which were yet to be constructed.[3] Kennedy Field was the place where Tuskegee Institute offered civilian pilot training before military flight training for black pilots began.

34

The misconception that the Tuskegee Airmen won the 1949 USAF gunnery meet in Las Vegas, defeating all other fighter groups in the Air Force

The fighter groups that took part in the USAF gunnery meet in Las Vegas competed in two categories. The jet aircraft category offered a total of one thousand points: four hundred for aerial gunnery, and two hundred each for ground gunnery, dive bombing, and skip bombing. The reciprocating (propeller) aircraft category offered a total of twelve hundred points: four hundred for aerial gunnery, and two hundred each for panel gunnery, dive bombing, skip bombing, and rockets. The 4th Fighter Group won the jet aircraft category, with 490.180 points, 49 percent of what was possible. The 332d Fighter Group won the reciprocating aircraft category, with 536.588 points, 45 percent of what was possible. It would not be fair to compare the fighter groups on the basis of total points, since the groups flying in the reciprocal class could earn two hundred points more than the groups flying in the jet class. While the 332d Fighter Group scored more points total than any other group, it was competing in a category that allowed two hundred points beyond that allowed for groups in the jet class. If one compares the fighter groups by the percentage of points they scored of the possible total, the 4th Fighter Group actually scored better. To compare the groups of the two different classes, however, would not be fair, since the categories were different, and the total number of points allowed was also different. In any case, it would be false to say that the 332d Fighter Group won the 1949 USAF gunnery meet and defeated all the other groups that competed.[1]

35

The misconception that Tuskegee Airman Daniel "Chappie" James was an ace

Sometimes people ask if Gen. Daniel "Chappie" James, the first black four-star general in the Air Force or in any of the American services, and a Tuskegee Airman who served during three different wars, World War II, Korea, and Vietnam, was an ace. The short answer is no. An ace is one who received credit for having shot down five enemy aircraft, and James has no aerial victory credits. While he served during World War II, he did not take part in combat during that war. While he served as a fighter pilot in both the Korean and Vietnam Wars, he did not shoot down any enemy aircraft in either of those conflicts.[1]

LaVone Kay of the Red Tail Squadron of the Commemorative Air Force, in an email she sent me on December 18, 2014, mentioned that someone at an airshow conference that same month had raised the question of whether Daniel "Chappie" James was "the first Tuskegee Airman Ace in Vietnam." I informed her that there were no Tuskegee Airmen aces, Gen. James did not earn any aerial victory credits, and one would need five in order to be an ace. How did the rumor begin that Gen. James had been an ace, in Vietnam or anywhere else?

A clue is in the book *Scrappy: Memoir of a U.S. Fighter Pilot in Korea and Vietnam*, in which Howard C. "Scrappy" Johnson mentions that "Chappie" James, with whom he had flown in Korea, told him one day that he was going to be interviewed for a radio show. Johnson listened to the program because he wanted to hear his friend. He was surprised that the radio announcer introduced "Chappie" James as a jet ace from the Korean War. He was disappointed that James did not correct the radio announcer, because Johnson knew that James had no aerial victory credits in Korea and normally did not even fly jets there.[2] There might have been other incidents in which James was introduced as an ace and did not correct the misperception.

36

The misconception that Tuskegee Airman Benjamin O. Davis Jr. graduated top in his class at the United States Military Academy at West Point

The Red Tail Squadron of the Commemorative Air Force produced a film about its restoration of a P-51 painted to look like an aircraft flown by the Tuskegee Airmen when they achieved fame as bomber escort pilots. The Red Tail Squadron has flown the airplane to remind people about the Tuskegee Airmen of World War II, a commendable endeavor. However, the film version shown in February 2015 contained two myths. It repeated the "never lost a bomber" claim already refuted in a previous section of this book. It also mentioned another myth I had never heard before: that Benjamin O. Davis Jr., the most famous Tuskegee Airman of all, had graduated top in his class at the U.S. Military Academy at West Point. I am not certain where that claim originated. Davis actually graduated 35th in his class of 276 at West Point, as he noted in his autobiography.[1] In other words, he graduated in the top 13 percent of his class. That is an outstanding record of achievement, especially given the discrimination of the times. During his time at the academy, other cadets shunned and ostracized him, but he persevered to become the first African American to graduate from West Point in the twentieth century and only the fourth to graduate from there in American history to that time.[2] Still, since he did not graduate in the top 10 percent of his class, it would be a misleading stretch to say that he graduated at the "top of his class," which many would interpret as first in his class.

37

The misconception that there were "second-generation Tuskegee Airmen"

Sometimes African American pilots who were not Tuskegee Airmen but who were portrayed as following in the footsteps of the Tuskegee Airmen have been erroneously called "second-generation Tuskegee Airmen." Two examples are Col. Roosevelt Lewis and Col. Richard (Dick) Toliver, both of whom became successful African American pilots in the U.S. Air Force who followed in the footsteps of the famous Tuskegee Airmen but were not Tuskegee Airmen themselves and were not sons of Tuskegee Airmen either. Lewis trained to fly with Charles Alfred "Chief" Anderson at Tuskegee, who had also provided civilian and primary military flight training to many if not most of the Tuskegee Airmen. Col. Lewis and Chief Anderson became close friends.[1]

The truth is that there were no second-generation Tuskegee Airmen. A second-generation Tuskegee Airman would have had to be a Tuskegee Airman and the son or daughter of a Tuskegee Airman. The Tuskegee Airmen served from 1941, when the first black flying unit came into existence, to 1949, when the last all-black flying unit was inactivated and the segregated Air Force ended. During those eight years, there were no Tuskegee Airmen whose sons or daughters were also Tuskegee Airmen.

To be sure, a great many black Air Force pilots who earned their wings after 1949 were inspired by the Tuskegee Airmen and followed in their footsteps. Although these African American servicemembers carried on the Tuskegee Airmen's pioneering work, they were not really second-generation Tuskegee Airmen because they were not the children of Tuskegee Airmen or Tuskegee Airmen themselves.

38

The misconception that each of the Tuskegee Airmen was awarded a Congressional Gold Medal or Medal of Honor

The highest individual honor for a military member is the Medal of Honor, which is awarded in the name of Congress. For that reason, it is sometimes called the Congressional Medal of Honor, when in fact it is the Medal of Honor. Sometimes that award is confused with the Congressional Gold Medal, which Congress sometimes orders to be created to honor an individual or a group, sometimes military and sometimes not. Congress awarded the Tuskegee Airmen the Congressional Gold Medal, not each Tuskegee Airman a Congressional Gold Medal, or a Medal of Honor, with which it is sometimes confused.

On April 11, 2006, Congress passed Public Law 109-213, which, according to section 2, called for "a single gold medal on appropriate design in honor of the Tuskegee Airmen, collectively, in recognition of their unique military record, which inspired revolutionary reform in the Armed Forces." The law also specifies that "the gold medal shall be given to the Smithsonian Institution, where it will be displayed as appropriate and made available for research."[1]

In March 2007, President George W. Bush presided over an impressive ceremony at which the Tuskegee Airmen were honored with the completed medal. Many Tuskegee Airmen attended this ceremony and were given bronze replicas of the gold medal, but the original gold medal remained in Washington, where it was placed on display at the Smithsonian Institution's National Air and Space Museum.[2] Later, the Congressional Gold Medal awarded to the Tuskegee Airmen was transferred to the National Museum of African American History and Culture, which opened in Washington, D.C., in late 2016.

In the years since 2007, people have sometimes been under the illusion that Congress had awarded a Congressional Gold Medal, or even the Medal of Honor, to each of the Tuskegee Airmen individually, and that if one of them was not at the ceremony at the Capitol to receive it, he or she deserved to get one too, possibly in another ceremony.[3] For example, in April 2015, Sgt. Amelia Jones was honored in a ceremony for her service with the Tuskegee Airmen during World War II. A newspaper article about the event announced in its headline: "95-year-old Tuskegee Air(wo)man receives Congressional Gold

Medal," as if Congress in 2015 awarded a Gold Medal to her as an individual. What she actually received was a bronze replica of the Congressional Gold Medal that had been awarded collectively to all the Tuskegee Airmen in 2007.[4] Another article, also published in April 2015, claimed that Tuskegee Airman Lt. Col. Leo Gray earned "the Congressional Medal of Honor from President George W. Bush in 2006."[5] The reporter no doubt confused the Congressional Gold Medal, which was awarded to the Tuskegee Airmen collectively in 2007, with the Medal of Honor. In reality, only one Congressional Gold Medal was produced to honor all the Tuskegee Airmen collectively, and it was not an individual award such as the Medal of Honor.

There were well over fourteen thousand Tuskegee Airmen, if one counts not only the pilots but also the navigators, bombardiers, radio operators, and gunners who trained in the bombardment squadrons, and all the ground personnel, including administrative, maintenance, support, training, medical, intelligence, and other personnel in their various military organizations. If Congress had awarded a gold medal to each of them, the cost would have been truly exorbitant, and there might have not been enough gold to go around. Congress did not award a Gold Medal to each of the Tuskegee Airmen. Other military units have also been honored with a Congressional Gold Medal, such as the Doolittle Raiders, but individual members of those units were not each awarded one.

Bronze replicas of the original Congressional Gold Medal authorized by Congress to honor the Tuskegee Airmen were also offered in 2007 by the U.S. Mint for purchase for anyone who wanted one, not just to Tuskegee Airmen. Many of the replicas have been purchased and given to individual Tuskegee Airmen who were not able to attend the 2007 ceremony in Washington. Even persons who were not Tuskegee Airmen could order replicas of the medal, as I did. I gave my bronze Tuskegee Airmen Gold Medal replica to the National World War II Museum for display at a new exhibit about the African American experience in World War II.[6]

In 1997, President Bill Clinton awarded the Medal of Honor to seven African American World War II veterans, six of them posthumously. They were the only black Medal of Honor winners from World War II. None of those recipients was a Tuskegee Airman. They were 1st Lt. Vernon Baker, S. Sgt. Edward A. Carter Jr., 1st Lt. John R. Fox, PFC Willy F. James Jr., S. Sgt. Ruben Rivers, 1st Lt. Charles L. Thomas, and Pvt. George Watson. There might have been Tuskegee Airmen who had the same names (there was a Tuskegee Airman also named George Watson), but the black Medal of Honor winners from World War II did not belong to the Army Air Forces.[7]

39

The misconception that when the Tuskegee Airmen returned to the United States after combat overseas, no one welcomed them

A common misconception about the Tuskegee Airmen is that when they returned to the United States after having taken part in combat overseas, no one welcomed them or expressed appreciation for the combat service they had just performed for their country. Such a misconception is connected to a common account that as soon as the Tuskegee Airmen arrived back in the United States, they were separated from the white personnel, reminding them that they were returning to a segregated environment and racial discrimination despite the heroic service for their country.

Not all the Tuskegee Airmen who returned from combat overseas were on the same ship or came back at the same time. Some of them returned during the war, after having completed the requisite number of combat missions. An example is Charles Dryden, a 99th Fighter Squadron pilot who returned even before the 332d Fighter Group deployed. Many others returned during the summer of 1945 after the war in Europe ended. They were on various ships along with other returning servicemen. Not all of them had the same experience when they got back to the United States.

Lt. Col. Leo Gray, pilot of a red-tailed P-51 who belonged to the 100th Fighter Squadron of the 332d Fighter Group, remembered that when his Liberty ship, the *Levi Woodbury*, arrived in New York on October 17, 1945, after having crossed the Atlantic Ocean to unload combat veterans from World War II such as him, there was a big welcome. Entertainment had been arranged, and there was a large crowd of well-wishers. The idea that none of the Tuskegee Airmen were ever welcomed upon returning home and shown appreciation for their military service overseas is false.[1]

40

The misconception that the Tuskegee Airmen were instrumental in the defeat of German forces in North Africa

On January 8, 2015, Dr. Russell Minton recorded a half-hour YouTube video in which he claimed to be telling "the real history of the Tuskegee Airmen." In the recording, Dr. Minton claimed that the Tuskegee Airmen, more than any other military entity, defeated German FM Erwin Rommel in North Africa by destroying hundreds of his tanks with P-39 airplanes. He claimed that the airmen were more instrumental in the Allied victory in North Africa than FM Bernard Montgomery, the Allied commander. Dr. Minton repeated the same claims in the spring of 2015 at Osceola High School in Kissimmee, Florida.[1] Dr. Minton was not speaking from his personal experience because he never deployed overseas or took part with the Tuskegee Airmen in combat. I do not believe he made up the claims he repeated but was passing on Tuskegee Airmen stories he had heard from others without checking the unit histories the Tuskegee Airmen wrote themselves during World War II to see if the stories were accurate.

The Tuskegee Airmen never fought Rommel or destroyed German tanks in North Africa. FM Erwin Rommel fought his last battle in North Africa on March 6, 1943. Gen. Jurgen von Arnim succeeded Rommel in charge of German and Italian forces in Tunisia, North Africa, on March 9, 1943. Gen. Armin surrendered all his forces in North Africa to Gen. Montgomery on May 12, 1943. Although the 99th Fighter Squadron, the only Tuskegee Airmen organization to deploy to North Africa, arrived in Morocco on April 24, 1943, it did not fly its first combat mission until June 2, 1943, approximately three weeks after all enemy forces surrendered in North Africa. Moreover, when the 99th Fighter Squadron began flying combat missions over North Africa from liberated Tunisia, it was flying P-40s, not P-39s, and the missions were to patrol Allied shipping in the Mediterranean and ward off enemy air attacks, not to destroy enemy tanks in North Africa.[2]

41

The misconception that all black personnel in the Army Air Forces during World War II were Tuskegee Airmen

The claim that all of the black personnel in the Army Air Forces during World War II, or even a majority of them, were Tuskegee Airmen is false. The total number of Tuskegee Airmen, including not only the pilots but also the many more personnel who were not pilots but who served in their units and at their bases, was more than fourteen thousand.[1] As many as two thousand more were not counted in previous listings, making the total as many as sixteen thousand. According to the Army Air Forces Statistical Digest published in 1946, which covered the World War II years, there were more than 145,000 black personnel in the Army Air Forces in December 1943 alone.[2] The total number of black personnel who served in the Army Air Forces during all the war years was much higher than that. The total number of Tuskegee Airmen who were black was probably no more than 10 percent of the total number of black personnel in the Army Air Forces during World War II.

Among the black personnel who belonged to the Army Air Forces who were not Tuskegee Airmen were the members of black aviation squadrons. More than 250 of such squadrons existed in 1944. The black aviation squadrons were not flying units but were labor organizations that served at bases all over the United States. Black Americans also served in other Army Air Forces units, including truck companies, medical and quartermaster units, and engineer aviation battalions, many of which served overseas in combat theaters around the world, the latter to construct and maintain forward air bases but not to fly airplanes. None of these were considered Tuskegee Airmen unless they served at the same bases where the Tuskegee Airmen served.[3]

42

The misconception that Tuskegee Airman Leo Gray flew the last mission in Europe during World War II

In an article by Jeff Jardine published on August 26, 2015, Tuskegee Airman Leo Gray is quoted as having claimed that he flew the last mission of the war in Europe on May 7, 1945.[1] That was the day the German high command surrendered unconditionally.[2]

The claim is questionable for a number of reasons. Leo Gray was flying with the 332d Fighter Group, which was assigned at the time to the 306th Fighter Wing. All of the composite mission reports of the 306th Fighter Wing for May 1945, including the one for May 7, note under the 332d Fighter Group the words "stand down." In other words, according to the documentation, the 332d Fighter Group flew no missions on that day or any other day in May 1945. The 332d Fighter Group histories and collected mission reports also do not show any mission flown on May 7, 1945.[3]

The same May 7, 1945, mission report of the 306th Fighter Wing shows that the 31st Fighter Group, the 52d Fighter Group, and the 325th Fighter Group, which also flew P-51 fighters in the wing, did fly missions that day. According to that report, the last missions of the wing were flown not by the 332d Fighter Group but by one of the other P-51 fighter groups of the 306th Fighter Wing.[4]

One may well ask why the three other P-51 groups in the 306th Fighter Wing of the Fifteenth Air Force have mission sorties listed in early May 1945, but the 332d Fighter Group does not. The 332d Fighter Group history for May 1945 suggests reasons. One reason could be that during the first week in that month, the 332d Fighter Group was moving from Ramitelli Airfield to Cattolica Airdrome, Italy, a fact confirmed in the group's lineage and honors history. The headquarters of the group completed its move to Cattolica around May 4, 1945. The three squadrons assigned to the group at the time, the 99th, 100th, and 301st, moved circa May 5, circa May 4, and circa May 4, respectively (the 302d Fighter Squadron had been inactivated on March 6). During the time the group was moving from one base to another, in early May, it would have had less chance to fly combat missions. It would have had to "stand down."[5]

If the group completed its move by May 4 or 5, could not missions have been flown by squadrons of the group on or after that day? It is a reasonable question. There is an answer in the group history for May 1945: "an armada of 'Red Tails' participated in the Fifteenth Air Force Review which took place over Caserta and Bari on 6 May 1945."[6] It is possible that Leo Gray flew in the aerial review on May 6 instead of on the last mission in Europe in World War II on May 7.

According to Kit C. Carter and Robert Mueller, who edited the book *The Army Air Forces in World War II Combat Chronology, 1941–1945*, the Ninth Air Force and the Twelfth Air Force flew missions in Europe on May 8, 1945, the day after the last missions flown by the 306th Fighter Wing of the Fifteenth Air Force. This source suggests that not only did Leo Gray of the 332d Fighter Group not fly the last mission in Europe during World War II, but neither did any of the other groups of the 306th Fighter Wing or of the Fifteenth Air Force.[7]

Leo Gray claimed that the last mission he flew in Europe, on May 7, was over the Brenner Pass between Italy and Austria, to test whether the Germans had ceased firing their antiaircraft weapons in the area. I have found no evidence of such a mission on that day, but I did find a report on an 82d Fighter Group mission over the Brenner Pass on May 12 or 13, 1945, after V-E Day. In that report is a note that with the 82d Fighter Group P-38s was a single P-51, an aircraft type not normally flown by the 82d Fighter Group. Is it possible that Gray flew in that P-51 over the Brenner Pass on May 12 or 13 but reported the wrong date, possibly because by May 12 or 13, the war was already over? The Fifteenth Air Force mission reports for May 1945 show several missions flown after V-E Day, which was May 8. Many of those other missions were of bombers dropping supplies over formerly occupied territory.[8]

This documentation does not support the claim that Tuskegee Airman Leo Gray flew the last mission in Europe during World War II.

43

The misconception that most black officers at Freeman Field, Indiana, in April 1945, refused to sign a new base regulation requiring segregated officers' clubs and were arrested as a result

Sometimes one reads or hears the story of the "Freeman Field Mutiny" told as if all or most black officers stationed at Freeman Field refused to sign a new base regulation requiring segregated officers' clubs and were arrested as a result.[1] The fact is that the great majority of black officers at Freeman Field at the time, April 1945, were not arrested, presumably because they did not refuse to obey an order to sign the new base regulation.

In April 1945, there were 422 black officers at Freeman Field. Col. Robert Selway, commander of the field and of the 477th Bombardment Group stationed there, required all the officers to sign a new base regulation requiring two segregated officers' clubs, one for trainers and one for trainees. The real purpose was to create separate officers' clubs for whites and blacks. The number of black officers who refused to sign the new regulation and were arrested for disobeying an order to sign it was 101. Sixty-one black officers had been arrested earlier for trying to enter the white officers' club at Freeman Field but fifty-eight of them had been released. Many of those 58 were among the 101 arrested for refusing to sign the new regulation. In other words, some of the black officers were arrested twice. The total number of black officers arrested at Freeman Field in April 1945 because of the segregated officers' clubs' policy was 120. That was less than 30 percent of the 422 black officers stationed at the base at the time. Assuming all those who disobeyed the order to sign the new base regulation were arrested, more than 70 percent of the black officers at Freeman Field signed the new base regulation, although many of them signed with objections.[2] The great majority of black officers at Freeman Field did not take part in the "mutiny."

44

The misconception that Tuskegee Airmen fighter or bomber pilots flew combat missions in Asia or the Pacific Theater during World War II or over Normandy during the D-Day invasion

I once viewed a wonderful exhibit of paintings of Tuskegee Airmen and their aircraft as they were during World War II. The paintings were superbly rendered, but one demonstrated another myth regarding the Tuskegee Airmen: that they flew fighter missions in Asia or the Pacific during World War II. The painting showed a red-tailed P-51 escorting a B-29 on a combat mission. B-29s were used in combat only in the China-Burma-India and Pacific Theaters of Operation during World War II and not in Europe. The Tuskegee Airmen never escorted B-29s in combat. The Tuskegee Airmen flew all their combat missions over North Africa, the Mediterranean Sea, Italy, and other parts of Europe.[1]

In the course of my work as a historian at the Air Force Historical Research Agency, I occasionally receive questions about the missions of the Tuskegee Airmen over Normandy on June 6, 1944, D-Day, when Allied forces invaded northern France. The Tuskegee Airmen combat pilots at the time were stationed at Ramitelli Air Base in Italy and had just begun flying bomber escort missions for the Fifteenth Air Force in June 1944. They could not fly missions over Normandy because they were based entirely too far away. It was the Eighth and Ninth Air Forces that were flying missions over Normandy on D-Day, and the Tuskegee Airmen never served with those numbered air forces, which were based at the time in England.[2]

During the summer of 1945 just after the war in Europe ended, the 477th Composite Group, also composed of Tuskegee Airmen, whose pilots were training with B-25 medium bombers, was preparing to deploy overseas for combat somewhere among the islands of the Pacific Ocean. The Japanese agreement to surrender in August, not long after the dropping of two atomic bombs over Hiroshima and Nagasaki, made that deployment unnecessary, and the 477th never went to the Pacific or flew combat missions there during World War II.[3]

45

The misconception that no Tuskegee Airmen pilots flew combat missions in the Pacific Theater during World War II

Sometimes individuals who know that no Tuskegee Airmen organizations and no Tuskegee Airmen fighter or bomber pilots flew any combat missions in the Pacific during World War II make the mistaken assumption that no Tuskegee Airmen pilots flew any combat missions in the Pacific during the war. They are forgetting that among the Tuskegee Airmen pilots were liaison pilots. Liaison pilots flew small airplanes with U.S. Army ground forces for artillery spotting, reconnaissance, communication, and other missions supporting the troops. The great majority of the black pilots who became liaison pilots during World War II trained at Tuskegee and are considered to be Tuskegee Airmen. There were fifty-one liaison pilots who trained at Tuskegee, and they served with various U.S. Army units all around the world. Some of those army units served in combat in the Pacific. According to Maj. Welton I. Taylor, one of the few black liaison pilots in World War II who did not train at Tuskegee, fourteen Tuskegee-trained liaison pilots served with him in the Pacific. Among them were 1st Lt. James Minor and 2d Lts. Charles Elam, Leander Hall, Darryl Bishop, and Sherman Smith.[1]

46

The misconception that the Tuskegee Airmen won the first Top Gun Competition

....

In misconception 34, I mentioned that the Tuskegee Airmen were not the only winners of the first USAF gunnery meet at Las Vegas in 1949. The 332d Fighter Group won the conventional or nonjet category, and the 4th Fighter Group won the jet aircraft category. There was no overall winner since the two categories had different numbers of events and the jet aircraft group winner did not compete with the conventional aircraft group winner. There were two winners, and it would be as accurate to say the 4th Fighter Group won the competition as it would to say the 332d Fighter Group did. Neither group won the overall competition because there was no overall winner.[1] But there is a further misconception that the Tuskegee Airmen were the first Top Gun winners.

The 1949 USAF gunnery meet in Las Vegas was not called "Top Gun." Calling the meet "Top Gun" confuses it with the much later official Top Gun competitions of the U.S. Navy, which started with a U.S. Navy F-4 squadron, VF-121, in 1969. The Top Gun competitions became formal at the U.S. Navy's Fighter Weapons School at Miramar, California, in 1972. Top Gun competitions later took place at the Naval Strike and Air Warfare Center at the same base. A 1986 Hollywood movie called *Top Gun* popularized the navy pilot competition, which stressed air-to-air combat skills. Calling the 1949 USAF gunnery meet "Top Gun" is very misleading, since it suggests the competition was an official U.S. Navy event and that it only tested air-to-air skills, when it was as much an air-to-ground as an air-to-air set of competitions.[2]

47

The misconception that the Tuskegee Airmen were among the victims of the infamous Tuskegee syphilis experiment that lasted from 1932 to 1972

Sometimes the Tuskegee Airmen experience has been called an "experiment" because some observers expected the first black pilots in military service to fail and regarded their training and entry into combat overseas as only a test. To many observers, the experience certainly proved the ability of black pilots to fly and fight as well as their white counterparts and demonstrated their equal ability. Some even claimed that the "experiment" proved that the black pilots could outperform others. Calling the Tuskegee Airmen experience an experiment, however, is problematic, because there was an infamous medical study going on at the same time at Tuskegee that was also called an experiment. There was no connection between the two.

In 1932, the Public Health Service, working with Tuskegee Institute, inaugurated the "Tuskegee Study of Untreated Syphilis in the Negro Male" in order to examine the effects of the disease. Participants in the study volunteered to receive free medical exams, free meals, and burial insurance, but those discovered to have syphilis were not told they had the disease, and they were not given effective medical treatment for syphilis because it was not available at the time. Effective treatment for syphilis became available in 1945, after the discovery of penicillin. Despite that, the study continued, and the black men in the Tuskegee medical study were not given penicillin or any other effective treatment. In 1972, the study was terminated as a result of public condemnation of the failure to treat those participants who were sick from the disease. There was even a lawsuit to punish those responsible.[1]

Since both the medical study and the Tuskegee Airmen experience have both been called experiments, and since both took place in part at Tuskegee, some people have developed the false idea that the Tuskegee Airmen were victims of the syphilis study. According to one article, a University of Kentucky researcher claimed that the forty-year syphilis study at Tuskegee involved the Tuskegee Airmen.[2] When I spoke about the Tuskegee Airmen in Mobile years ago, an audience member even claimed that the Tuskegee Airmen had been injected with syphilis to cause them to fail.[3] Such a claim is absurd. The

Tuskegee Airmen experience was totally separate from the Tuskegee syphilis study, and the Tuskegee Airmen were a totally separate set of individuals from those who were involved as study volunteers. The study, which began in 1932, almost ten years before the Tuskegee Airmen came into existence in 1941, concluded in 1972, twenty-three years after the Tuskegee Airmen experience ended.

48

The misconception that the Tuskegee Airmen were called the Tuskegee Airmen during World War II

I have found no World War II documents regarding the first black pilots in American military service, who all served with the Army Air Forces, that refers to them as the "Tuskegee Airmen." They were called members of their units, such as the 99th Fighter Squadron or the 332d Fighter Group, or the "Red Tails" after the color of the tails of the 332d Fighter Group's P-51s between July 1944 and May 1945. The term "Tuskegee Airmen" was probably invented by Charles Francis, who titled his 1955 book about them *The Tuskegee Airmen*. He called them that because the pilots had trained to fly at Tuskegee. After publication of that book, the term became popular among the black pilot veterans, who began to refer to themselves as the Tuskegee Airmen, and later developed an organization, the Tuskegee Airmen Incorporated, to preserve their legacy and promote education.[1]

49

The misconception that the Tuskegee Airmen were a squadron

In many publications I have seen the Tuskegee Airmen referred to as a squadron, as if all the black pilots in the Army Air Forces during World War II belonged to one squadron. Mary Doll of the National Park Service brought a recent case to my attention when handling a memorial in North Carolina in March 2018, but I had encountered the same statement in many other places earlier.[1] The Tuskegee Airmen belonged to a great many organizations. The pilots belonged to one of eight squadrons, or to one of the two groups to which the squadrons were assigned. They were the 99th, 100th, 301st, and 302d Fighter Squadrons of the 332d Fighter Group and the 616th, 617th, 618th, and 619th Fighter Squadrons of the 477th Fighter Group.[2] There was also another fighter squadron, the 553d, to which newly trained pilots were assigned before deployment overseas. There were at least eleven organizations to which the pilots were assigned. In addition to those eleven, there were many other Tuskegee Airmen units to which ground personnel were assigned to support the training of the black pilots or to maintain and repair their aircraft on the ground.

50

The misconception that the Tuskegee Airmen flew more than fifteen thousand missions during World War II

Sometimes people unfamiliar with military aviation terminology confuse missions with sorties and claim that the Tuskegee Airmen flew more than fifteen thousand missions during World War II, when in fact they flew more than fifteen thousand sorties. One mission of the 332d Fighter Group might have included many aircraft. Each aircraft taking off and returning to base would comprise a sortie, but together they would have flown one mission. For example, on July 4, 1944, forty-seven P-51s of the 332d Fighter Group took off for a bomber escort mission. The Tuskegee Airmen flew one mission that day, but they had forty effective sorties. On July 7, the 332d Fighter Group flew one mission, and fifty-one P-51s took off to fly it. The Tuskegee Airmen flew one mission that day, but they had fifty-one sorties. When the 99th Fighter Squadron flew missions for the Twelfth Air Force in 1943, sometimes only two or a few aircraft took part in a mission. Still, the number of sorties outnumbered the number of missions. During World War II, the Tuskegee Airmen flew close to fifteen hundred missions but more than fifteen thousand sorties.[1]

51

The misconception that the Tuskegee Airmen were the first African American military pilots

The Tuskegee Airmen were the first African American pilots in U.S. military service, but they were not the first African American pilots in military service generally. At least five African American pilots served in the military services of other countries before African American pilots could serve in the American armed services. During World War I, Eugene Bullard flew in the French Air Service. Two African American pilots, Hubert Julian and John C. Robinson, served in the armed forces of Ethiopia in 1935 and 1936. In fact, Robinson served as head of the Imperial Ethiopian Air Force in 1936 as Ethiopia resisted Italian conquest. Two other African American pilots, James Lincoln Holt Peck and Paul Williams, served in the Republican Army Air Force of Spain in 1937 during the Spanish Civil War.[1]

52

The misconception that General Daniel "Chappie" James graduated from the Tuskegee Institute in 1942

Short biographies of Tuskegee Airman Gen. Daniel "Chappie" James Jr., the first black four-star general in United States military service, sometimes state that he received his college degree from the Tuskegee Institute in 1942.[1] Even official short USAF biographies of Gen. James have incorrectly stated this. In reality, when General James was a student at Tuskegee Institute in 1941, during his fourth academic year, not long before he would have graduated, he was expelled for fighting. Immediately after his expulsion, he began working with the black civilian flight instructors at the primary flight school that the Tuskegee Institute ran at Moton Field, but he did not receive his college degree from that institution in that decade or the next. In fact, he did not receive his college degree from Tuskegee Institute until 1969, just before he was promoted from the rank of colonel to brigadier general, partly because a college degree was a prerequisite for promotion to general. Tuskegee Institute leaders awarded then Col. Daniel James Jr. his bachelor of science degree in physical education partly because of the non–Tuskegee Institute courses he had taken while he was in the Air Force in the intervening twenty-seven or twenty-eight years between his expulsion and his graduation.[2]

53

The misconception that most Tuskegee Airmen were pilots

While the most famous of the Tuskegee Airmen were pilots, the overwhelming majority of them were not. The Tuskegee Airmen Incorporated's Harry Sheppard Historical Research Committee maintains a database originally compiled by Ted Johnson that lists documented original Tuskegee Airmen. This list contains more than fourteen thousand names. The number of Tuskegee Airmen pilots was approximately one thousand. That means that for every Tuskegee Airman pilot, at least thirteen Tuskegee Airmen were not pilots. They included maintenance personnel; staff personnel; armorers; transportation, communication, and weather personnel; training personnel; intelligence personnel; and other ground personnel, many of whom were not officers. Only a minority of the Tuskegee Airmen were pilots.[1]

54

The misconception that white pilots in the Army Air Forces of World War II could go home after fifty missions but black pilots could not

Before 1944, various numbered air forces of the Army Air Forces experimented with policies of limiting the number of missions that bomber crews would be expected to fly before allowing them to go home. Those policies varied but were dropped by the time the Tuskegee Airmen started escorting Fifteenth Air Force bomber crews from Italian bases in the middle of 1944. Not only was there no policy by then of sending the bomber crews home after fifty missions, but there had not been a policy of limiting the missions of the fighter escort pilots even when there had been a limit to the number of missions for the bomber crews. Moreover, the black fighter pilots of the 332d Fighter Group were not the only fighter pilots in the Fifteenth Air Force. Six other fighter escort groups were in the Fifteenth Air Force, all of them white. None of those fighter pilots, black or white, could go home after flying fifty missions, and both black and white pilots often flew well over fifty missions during the war. There was no policy of letting the white pilots go home after fifty missions and making the black pilots fly more than fifty when black and white pilots were flying together on missions in the Fifteenth Air Force during World War II between early June 1944 and the end of April 1945. By mid-1944, none of the numbered air forces, including the Eighth Air Force in England, had a policy of sending bomber crews or pilots home after fifty missions, even though early in the war, the bomber crews could go home after a set number of missions. That policy had been abandoned for all pilots and crews by the middle of 1944, when the Tuskegee Airmen began flying their bomber escort missions.

Col. Donald Blakeslee, a white fighter pilot in World War II, flew nearly five hundred fighter missions. Harold S. Snow, another white fighter pilot, flew one hundred missions in World War II.[1]

55

The misconception that the German fighter threat to Fifteenth Air Force bombers did not diminish significantly until after the Tuskegee Airmen began escorting them

Before the Allies invaded Normandy in early June 1944, they were determined to have control of the skies by reducing the Luftwaffe. During the first five months of 1944, the German fighter force lost 2,262 fighter pilots out of the 2,395 who had been on duty when the year started. During Operation Big Week, February 20–25, 1944, the Eighth Air Force and the Royal Air Force in England attacked German aircraft industries, partly to reduce German aircraft production but also to lure German fighters out to attack the American bombers so that the P-51 and P-47 escorts for those fighters could shoot them down. Hundreds of German fighter interceptors were shot down by the escorts and the bombers, and possibly hundreds of skilled German fighter pilots lost their lives. The Luftwaffe lost more than a third of its authorized strength that February.[1] In May 1944, the Luftwaffe lost a quarter of its fighter pilots. By June 1944, when the Tuskegee Airmen began escorting heavy bombers of the Fifteenth Air Force, the Luftwaffe fighter threat had already diminished greatly and was concentrating in the northwest to counter the invasion and the threats of the Eighth and Ninth Air Forces in England. The Germans devoted fewer aircraft to the threat from the Twelfth and Fifteenth Air Forces in Italy. Many of the experienced German fighter pilots had already been lost, and their less experienced replacements lacked the training and experience of their predecessors. The Germans lacked the fuel for adequate training flights. A great majority of the daily narrative mission reports of the 332d Fighter Group covering the period June 1944 through April 1945 indicate that no enemy aircraft were encountered. The Tuskegee Airmen reported enemy aircraft encounters on only 35 of the 179 bomber escort missions they flew for the Fifteenth Air Force.[2] The idea that the loss rate of American bombers to enemy aircraft did not go down significantly until the 332d Fighter Group began escorting Fifteenth Air Force heavy bombers, in June 1944, is not accurate.[3]

Conclusion

Whoever dispenses with the misconceptions that have come to circulate around the Tuskegee Airmen in the many decades since World War II emerges with a greater appreciation for what they actually accomplished. If they did not demonstrate that they were far superior to the members of the six non-black fighter escort groups of the Fifteenth Air Force with which they served, they certainly demonstrated that they were not inferior to them. Moreover, the Tuskegee Airmen began at a line farther back, overcoming many more obstacles on the way to combat. The Tuskegee Airmen proved that they were equal to the other fighter pilots with whom they served heroically during World War II. Their exemplary performance contributed to the fact that of all the military services, the Air Force was the first to integrate in 1949.

Daniel L. Haulman, PhD

Notes

Misconception 1

1. Alan L. Gropman, *The Air Force Integrates, 1945–1964* (Washington, D.C.: Office of Air Force History, 1985), 2–3.

2. Gropman, *The Air Force Integrates*, 12; Ulysses Lee, *The Employment of Negro Troops* (Washington, D.C.: Office of the Chief of Military History, United States Army, 1966), 157.

3. Air Force Historical Research Agency (AFHRA), call number 134.65-496.

4. USAF Historical Study No. 85, "USAF Credits for the Destruction of Enemy Aircraft, World War II" (Washington, D.C.: Office of Air Force History, 1978); Maurer Maurer, *Air Force Combat Units of World War II* (Washington, D.C.: Office of Air Force History, 1983).

5. Army Air Forces Statistical Digest for World War II, 1946 (Washington, D.C.: Statistical Control Division, Office of Air Comptroller, June 1947), 256 (table 160).

Misconception 2

1. Alan L. Gropman, *The Air Force Integrates, 1945–1964* (Washington, D.C.: Office of Air Force History, 1985), 14.

2. Daniel L. Haulman, "Tuskegee Airmen-Escorted Bombers Lost to Enemy Aircraft," paper prepared at the Air Force Historical Research Agency. This paper is based on histories of the 332d Fighter Group, daily mission reports of the Fifteenth Air Force, and Missing Air Crew Reports that show the times, locations, and causes of aircraft losses.

3. Interview of General Benjamin O. Davis Jr., by Alan Gropman, Air Force Historical Research Agency (AFHRA), call number K239.0512-122.

4. Fifteenth Air Force General Order 2972 issued on August 31,1944.

5. 332d Fighter Group histories, call number GP-332-HI ; Fifteenth Air Force daily mission folders, AFHRA, call number 670.332; Missing Air Crew Reports, indexed and filed on microfiche in the Archives Branch of the AFHRA.

Misconception 3

1. Oliver North, War Stories III (Washington, D.C.: Regnery Publishing, Inc., 2005), 152.

2. Interview of Lee Archer by Dr. Lisa Bratton, conducted on March 13, 2001, in New York, N.Y., on file at the Air Force Historical Research Agency (AFHRA), call number K239.0512-2580, 23–24.

3. Monthly histories of the 332d Fighter Group, June 1944–April 1945; Fifteenth Air Force General Order 2350, August 6, 1944; Fifteenth Air Force General Order 4287 November 1, 1944.

4. 332d Fighter Group narrative mission report 37, July 26, 1944.

5. Fifteenth Air Force General Order 2350 August 6, 1944.

6. Charles E. Francis, The Tuskegee Airmen (Boston: Bruce Humphries, Inc., 1955), 92, 194; 332d Fighter Group mission report 30, July 20, 1944.

7. Interview of Archer, by Bratton, 23–24; conversations between Daniel Haulman and Frank Olynyk during several of the latter's research visits to the Air Force Historical Research Agency.

8. "Dr. Russell Minton, 87, Talks about the Real History of the Tuskegee Airmen," You-Tube video of Dr. Russell Minton, recorded in January 2015, https://www.youtube .com/watch?v=16-4veOJFC4; histories of the 99th, 100th, 301st, and 302d Fighter Squadrons and the 332d Fighter Group during World War II; Twelfth and Fifteenth Air Force general orders awarded aerial victory credits during World War II, as shown on table 4.]

9. 332d Fighter Group histories for July and October 1944, AFHRA, call number GP-332-HI.

Misconception 4

1. John J. Kruzel, "President, Congress Honor Tuskegee Airmen," American Forces Press Service, March 30, 2007.

2. Interview of Lee Archer by Dr. Lisa Bratton, March 13, 2001,New York, N.Y., on file at the Air Force Historical Research Agency, call number K239.0512-2580, pp. 19–20.

3. Fifteenth Air Force General Order 2293, April 12, 1945.

4. USAAF (European Theater) Credits for the Destruction of Enemy Aircraft in Air-to-Air Combat, World War 2, Victory List No. 5, Frank J. Olynyk, May 1987; USAAF (Mediterranean Theater) Credits for the Destruction of Enemy Aircraft in Air-to-Air Combat, World War 2, Victory List No. 6, Frank J. Olynyk, June 1987; USAF Historical Study No. 85, USAF Credits for the Destruction of Enemy Aircraft, World War II, Albert F. Simpson Historical Research Center, 1978; Combat Squadrons of the Air Force, World War II, edited by Maurer Maurer, 1969.
Air Force Combat Units of World War II, edited by Maurer Maurer, 1983. This information was compiled by Ms. Patsy Robertson, a historian at the Air Force Historical Research Agency.

5. John B. Holway, *Red Tails, Black Wings* (Las Cruces, N.Mex.: Yucca Tree Press, 1997), 262.

6. Fifteenth Air Force General Orders 2525 and 2709, April 19, 1945, and April 24, 1945, respectively.

Misconception 5

1. 332d Fighter Group history for June 1944 and 332d Fighter Group mission report for June 25, 1944.

2. 332d Fighter Group history for June 1944 and 332d Fighter Group mission report for June 25, 1944; Interview of Lee Archer by Dr. Lisa Bratton, March 13, 2011, New York, N.Y., on file at the Air Force Historical Research Agency, call number K239.0512-2580, p. 20.

3. 332d Fighter Group history for June 1944; 332d Fighter Group mission report for 25 June 1944; David Brown, Warship Losses of World War II (Annapolis, Md: Naval Institute Press, 1990); "Fighting Ships of the World," website of Ivan Gogin, http://

www.navypedia.org/ships/germany/ger_tb_ta22.htm; Aldo Fraccaroli, Italian War-ships of World War II (London: Ian Allan, 1968). Jurgen Rohwer, Chronology of the War at Sea (London: Chatham Publishing, 2005), 338.

4. Charles Francis, *The Tuskegee Airmen*, 113–114; Fifteenth Air Force General Order 287, January 19, 1945; Fifteenth Air Force General Order 3950, October 15, 1944.

5. Myth contained in Wikipedia under Ariete Class Torpedo Boat; more correct infor-mation from H. P. Willmott's *The Last Century of Sea Power*, vol. 2, *From Washington to Tokyo, 1922–1945* (Bloomington: Indiana University Press, 2010), 207.

Misconception 6

1. J. Todd Moye, Freedom Flyers: The Tuskegee Airmen of World War II (New York: Oxford University Press, 2010), 121; John B. Holway, Red Tails, Black Wings (Las Cruces, N.Mex.: Yucca Tree Press, 1997), 260.

2. Lawrence P. Scott and William M. Womack Sr., Double V: The Civil Rights Struggle of the Tuskegee Airmen (East Lansing: Michigan State University Press, 1994), 225. The sources were interviews with Omar Blair, Woodrow Crockett, and George Watson.

3. 55th Air Service Squadron histories for December 1944–March 1945, Air Force His-torical Research Agency (AFHRA), call number SQ-SV-55-HI July 1942–May 1945.

4. Email from James Sheppard, an original Tuskegee Airmen and a member of the Tuskegee Airmen Incorporated, with whom the author has spoken and corresponded.

5. Holway, Red Tails, Black Wings, 260.

6. "Dr. Russell Minton, 87, Talks about the Real History of the Tuskegee Airmen," You-Tube video of Dr. Russell Minton, recorded in January 2015, https://www.youtube.com/watch?v-16-4veOJFC4.

7. Fifteenth Air Force daily mission reports, June and July 1944, AFHRA, call number 670.332.

8. Narrative Mission Reports of the 31st, 52d, 82d, 325th, and 332d Fighter Groups, contained in the Fifteenth Air Force mission folder for March 24, 1945, AFHRA, call number 670.332.

9. 55th Air Service Squadron history for March 1945. The AFHRA call number is SQ-SV-55-HI July 1942–May 1945.

10. Zellie Orr, Heroes in War- Heroes at Home (Marietta, Ga.: Communication Unlim-ited, 2008), 2–3.

11. Organization record cards of the 96th, 523d, and 524th Air Service Groups, and organization record card of the 366th Air Service Squadron, AFHRA..

12. Interview of Lee Archer by Dr. Lisa Bratton, in New York, N.Y., on March 13, 2001, AFHRA, call number K239.0512-2580, p. 19.

13. Documentation supplied by Craig Huntly, including a March 25, 1945, letter of commendation from Col. Benjamin O. Davis Jr. to the commander of the 366th Air Service Squadron, noting Capt. O. D. Blair, and a June 6, 1945, letter of commen-dation from Capt. Omar Blair to S. Sgt. George Watson for his role in obtaining the fuel tanks for the Berlin mission.

Misconception 7

1. John Holway, Red Tails and Black Wings (Las Cruces, N.Mex..: Yucca Tree Press, 1997), 249; Chris Bucholtz, 332d Fighter Group – Tuskegee Airmen (Oxford, UK: Osprey Publishing, 2007), 116.

2. Noel F. Parrish, "The Segregation of Negroes in the Army Air Forces," Air Command and Staff College thesis, Air University, Maxwell Air Force Base, May 1947, Air Force Historical Research Agency (AFHRA), call number 239.04347, May 1947, Parrish, 41.

3. Noel F. Parrish, "The Segregation of Negroes in the Army Air Forces," Air Command and Staff College thesis, Air University, Maxwell Air Force Base, May 1947, AFHRA, call number 239.04347, 39.

4. World War II statistical abstract; daily mission reports of the Fifteenth Air Force and the 332d Fighter Group between June 1944 and the end of April 1945; missing air crew reports of bombers shot down in the Fifteenth Air Force organizations in the same time period.

5. Kai Wright, Soldiers of Freedom: An Illustrated History of African Americans in the Armed Forces (New York: Black Dog and Leventhal Publishers, 2002), 181.

6. James H. Doolittle and Carroll V. Glines, I Could Never Be So Lucky Again (Atglen, Pa.: Schiffer Military/Aviation History, 1991), 380.

7. History of the Fifteenth Air Force, November 1943–May 1945, vol. I (Air Force Historical Research Agency call number 670.01-1), 277 and 286.

8. History of the 52d Fighter Group, May 1944, AFHRA, call number GP-52-HI, May 1944.

9. History of the Fifteenth Air Force, November 1943–May 1945, vol. I, AFHRA, call number 670.01-1, pp. 286–287.

10. Maurer Maurer, Air Force Combat Units of World War II (Washington, D.C.: Office of Air Force History, 1983), under each group designation.

11. Fifteenth Air Force mission folder for December 29, 1944; 485th Bombardment Group history for January 1945.

12. Ryan Orr, "Veteran's Life Saved by Tuskegee Airman," Victorville Daily Press, November 10, 2008; 332d Fighter Group histories for May, June, and July 1944; 31st Fighter Group history for May 1944; Fifteenth Air Force Daily Mission Folder for May 5, 1955; E. A. Munday, Fifteenth Air Force Combat Markings, 1943–1945 (London, UK: Beaumont Publications), 15–18.

13. Pete Mecca, "Tuskegee Airmen Assured Fellow Pilots a Happy New Year," The Covington News, January 1, 2014.

14. USAF Historical Study 85, USAF Credits for the Destruction of Enemy Aircraft, World War II (Washington, D.C.: Office of Air Force History, 1978); Maurer Maurer, Air Force Combat Units of World War II (Washington, D.C.: Office of Air Force History, 1983); email message from Barrett Tillman regarding Fifteenth Air Force aces.

15. Narrative mission reports of the 332d Fighter Group filed with the monthly histories of the 332d Fighter Group at the AFHRA for the period June 1944–April 1945.

There are 311 such narrative mission reports filed, but only 179 of these were bomber escort missions.

Misconception 8

1. Lineage and honors histories of the 99th Fighter Squadron, the 332d Fighter Group, and the 477th Bombardment Group, and their monthly histories from World War II, stored at the Air Force Historical Research Agency (AFHRA).

2. hotograph of 96th Service Group personnel, and table of personnel statistics of XV Service Command personnel per group by race and rank, provided by Craig Huntly to Daniel Haulman, January 9, 2017.

3. History of Tuskegee Army Flying School and AAF 66th FTD, book published by Wings of America, AFHRA, call number 289.28-100.

4. Conversations of the author with various original Tuskegee Airmen that took place during his attendance at five successive Tuskegee Airmen Incorporated national conventions in 2007, 2008, 2009, 2010, and 2011.

5. Alan L. Gropman, The Air Force Integrates (Washington, D.C.: Office of Air Force History 1985), 12–14 and 17–18.

6. History of Tuskegee Army Flying School and AAF 66th FTD, book published by Wings of America, AFHRA, call number 289.28-100; Robert J. Jakeman, The Divided Skies (Tuscaloosa: University of Alabama Press, 1992), 264–265; Lineage and honors history of the Fifty-Third Test and Evaluation Group (formerly the 79th Fighter Group) at the AFHRA.

7. Author's personal conversations with Tuskegee Airmen George Hardy and William Holloman, and with journalist Ron Brewington; articles announcing the death of Eugene Smith as a Tuskegee Airman, November 2012, including WCPO news site, Cincinnati, Ohio, November 26, 2012, and Eagle Radio 99.3 FM website, Lawrenceburg, Ind., November 26, 2012; Vevay Newspapers Online, November 29, 2012, "Eugene Smith, County Resident and Tuskegee Airman, Passes Away."

Misconception 9

1. Charles W. Dryden, A-Train: Memoirs of a Tuskegee Airman (Tuscaloosa: University of Alabama Press, 1997), 144–147.

2. Lineage and honors histories of the 99th Flying Training Squadron (formerly 99th Fighter Squadron) and 332d Expeditionary Operations Group (formerly 332d Fighter Group) at the Air Force Historical Research Agency (AFHRA), in addition to their monthly histories from 1943–1945.

3. 477th Fighter Group (formerly 477th Bombardment Group) lineage and honors history, and monthly histories of the 477th Bombardment Group in 1944 and 1945, at the AFHRA.

Misconception 10

1. Conversations of the author with several of the original Tuskegee Airmen at a series of five Tuskegee Airmen Incorporated national conventions between 2007 and 2011.

2. Robert J. Jakeman, The Divided Skies (Tuscaloosa: The University of Alabama Press,

1992), 221; Maurer Maurer, Combat Squadrons of the Air Force, World War II (Washington, D.C.: United States Government Printing Office, 1969), 329.

3. Information from Cheryl Ferguson of Tuskegee University archives, received on December 13, 2011.

4. Lewis Gould, American First Ladies: Their Lives and Their Legacy (Routledge, 2014), 294.

Misconception 11

1. Information from Dr. Roscoe Brown, telephone conversation with Dr. Daniel Haulman on December 13, 2011.

Misconception 12

1. James H. Doolittle and Carol V. Glines, I Could Never Be So Lucky Again (Atglen, Pa.: Schiffer Military Aviation History, 1991), 380.

Misconception 13

1. Interview of Lee Archer by Dr. Lisa Bratton, March 13, 2001, 2001, New York, N.Y., Air Force Historical Research Agency (AFHRA), call number K239.0512-2580, 19.

2. Fifteenth Air Force mission folder for March 24, 1945, which includes all the fighter group narrative mission reports for the day, AFHRA, call number 670.332; Fifteenth Air Force Field Order 159, March 23, 1945, for the March 24, 1945 mission to Berlin. The order noted that the XV Fighter Command was to provide five groups for strong escort for the 5th Bombardment Wing (AFHRA, call number 670.327, Mar–Apr 1945). The mission reports of the fighter groups confirm that five groups provided escort that day for the 5th Bombardment Wing that flew to Berlin.

Misconception 14

1. Maurer Maurer, Combat Squadrons of the Air Force, World War II (Washington, D.C.: Office of Air Force History, 1969), 329–330. The 99th Fighter Squadron was attached to four different white P-40 groups in the Mediterranean Theater before it joined the 332d Fighter Group and flew the same kinds of aircraft they did on the same kinds of missions.

2. Maurer Maurer, Combat Squadrons of the Air Force, World War II (Washington, D.C.: Department of the Air Force, 1969), 230, 233–235, 329–330; Charles E. Francis, The Tuskegee Airmen: The Men Who Changed a Nation (Wellesley, Mass.: Branden Books, 2008), 75.

3. War Department General Order 23, March 24, 1944; War Department General Order 76, September 8, 1945.

4. Interview of Col. Philip G. Cochran by James Hasdorff, Air Force Historical Research Agency(AFHRA), call number K239.0512-876, p. 122.

5. Gail Buckley, American Patriots (New York: Random House, 2001), 288.

6. "Dr. Russell Minton, 87, Talks about the Real History of the Tuskegee Airmen," YouTube video of Dr. Russell Minton, recorded in January 2015, https://www.youtube.com/watch?v=16-4veOJFC4.

7. Benjamin O. Davis Jr., Benjamin O. Davis, Jr, American (Washington, D.C.: Smithsonian Institution Press, 1991), 96.

Misconception 15

1. Robert J. Jakeman, The Divided Skies (Tuscaloosa: University of Alabama Press, 1992); J. Todd Moye, Freedom Flyers (Oxford, UK: Oxford University Press, 2010); History of Tuskegee Army Flying School, Air Force Historical Research Agency (AFHRA), call number 289.28-100.

2. Interview of Col. Philip G. Cochran by James Hasdorff, AFHRA, call number K239.0512-876, 124.

3. Lynn M. Homan and Thomas Reilly, Black Knights: The Story of the Tuskegee Airmen (Gretna, La.: Pelican Publishing Company, 2006), 105.

Misconception 16

1. Corey Bridwell and Paige Osburn, "Tuskegee Airmen's Legacy Celebrated at Compton's Tomorrow's Aeronautical Museum," KPCC, January 19, 2012; Robert Roten, "Laramie Movie Scope: Red Tails," http://www.lariat.org/AT The Movies/new /redtails.html; Sundiata Cha-Jua, "Red Tails, A Historically Accurate Film?"

2. Author's visit to the National Museum of the United States Air Force in early 2012, where he viewed the trophy for the Las Vegas gunnery meets of 1949–1950 and the panel describing the trophy and the competition; copy of the names on the plate of the United States Air Force Gunnery Award, forwarded from Dr. Jeffery S. Underwood of the National Museum of the United States Air Force to Daniel L. Haulman as an email attachment on May 7, 2012.

3. Email from Brett Stolle, curator of the National Museum of the USAF to Daniel Haulman of the Air Force Historical Research Agency, August 7, 2017.

4. National Museum of the United States Air Force Aircraft Catalog, edited by John King, 2011; Organization Record card of the National Museum of the United States Air Force, formerly the Air Force Museum and later the United States Air Force Museum, at the Air Force Historical Research Agency; Message from Dr. Jeffery S. Underwood of the National Museum of the United States Air Force to Daniel L. Haulman, May 7, 2012.

5. Email correspondence on August 9–10, 2017, between Daniel Haulman and curators at both the National Air and Space Museum and the National Museum of the United States Air Force, including Alex Spencer and Brett Stolle.

Misconception 17

1. "Desegregation of the Armed Forces," Harry S. Truman Library and Museum, http://www.trumanlibrary.org/whistlestop/study_collections/desegregation/large /index.php.

2. George Hardy, chairman of the Harry Sheppard Historical Research Committee of the Tuskegee Airmen Incorporated; Alan L. Gropman, The Air Force Integrates (Washington, D.C.: Office of Air Force History, 1985), 45–46, 55, 87–90.

3. Gropman, The Air Force Integrates, 1945–1964, 87–89,295; Letter, Spaatz to Graves, April 5, 1948, in Special File 35, Negro Affairs, 1948, Secretary of the Air Force, National Archives Record Group 340; John T. Correll, "The Air Force, 1907–2007," Air Force Magazine (September 2007); George Hardy, chairman of the Harry A. Sheppard Historical Research Committee.

Misconception 18

1. John B. Holway, *Red Tails: An Oral History of the Tuskegee Airmen* (Minneola, N.Y.: Dover Publications, 2011), 146

2. "Friendly Aircraft Markings," contained in a folder, "Lead Check List," among the documents of the Fifteenth Air Force, Air Force Historical Research Agency(AFHRA), call number 670.328-1, and correspondence between Daniel Haulman and Ron Spriggs that included testimony from Mr. James T. Sheppard, who maintained aircraft of the 332d Fighter Group at Ramitelli Air Field in Italy during World War II.

Misconception 19

1. Stanley Sandler, "Tuskegee Airmen," in *Ethnic and Racial Minorities in the U.S. Military: An Encyclopedia*, edited by Alexander Bielakowski (Santa Barbara, Calif.: ABC-CLIO, 2013), vol. II, 691–692.

2. Robert J. Jakeman, *The Divided Skies* (Tuscaloosa: The University of Alabama Press, 1992), 270–271; J. Todd Moye, *Freedom Flyers* (Oxford, UK: Oxford University Press, 2010), 83.

Misconception 20

1. James Doolittle, I Could Never Be So Lucky Again (Atglen, Pa.: Schiffer Military/ Aviation History, 1995), 380.

2. AAF Field Manual 1–15, Tactics and Techniques of Air Fighting, April 10, 1942.

3. Benjamin O. Davis Jr., Benjamin O. Davis, Jr., American (Washington, D.C.: Smithsonian Institution Press, 1991), 118, 122–123.

4. Letter, Gen. Henry "Hap" Arnold to Gen. George C. Marshall, November 3, 1943, Air Force Historical Research Agency(AFHRA).

5. Letter, Gen. Henry "Hap" Arnold to Maj. Gen. James H. Doolittle, December 25, 1943.

6. Doolittle, I Could Never Be So Lucky Again, 380.

7. Richard G. Davis, Carl A. Spaatz and the Air War in Europe (Washington, D.C.: Center for Air Force History, 1993), 319, 394.

Misconception 21

1. Author's visit to Enlisted Heritage Hall, Gunter Annex, Maxwell Air Force Base, June 8, 2013.

2. Lineage and honors histories of the 332d Fighter Group and its four squadrons, the 99th, 100th, 301st, and 302d Fighter Squadrons, on file at the Air Force Historical Research Agency (AFHRA) at Maxwell Air Force Base.

3. Lineage and honors histories of the 8th Fighter Group and its four fighter squadrons during World War II (the 35th, 36th, and 80th), contained in Maurer Maurer, Air

Force Combat Units of World War II (Washington, D.C.: Office of Air Force History, 1983); and Maurer Maurer, Combat Squadrons of the Air Force, World War II (Washington, D.C.: USAF Historical Division, Air University, 1969).

4. Lineage and Honors history of the 1st Air Commando Group, contained in Maurer, *Air Force Combat Units*, 19, and research by Barry Spink of the AFHRA.

Misconception 22

1. Maurer Maurer, Combat Squadrons of the Air Force, World War II (Washington, D.C.: USAF Historical Division, Air University, Department of the Air Force, 1969), 314–316, 329–330, 372–374.

2. Maurer Maurer, Air Force Combat Units of World War II (Washington, D.C.: Office of Air Force History, 1983), 21–24, 83–85, 212–213.

Misconception 23

1. Victor Barbosa, "Roscoe Brown: a True American Hero," Springfield Student, February 14, 2013.

2. Charles E. Francis, The Tuskegee Airmen: The Men Who Changed a Nation (1955; reprint, Boston: Branden Books, 2008).

3. Tuskegee Airmen Incorporated Membership Directory, July 2010, 1.

4. Joseph Caver, Jerome Ennels, and Daniel Haulman, The Tuskegee Airmen: An Illustrated History, 1939–1949 (Montgomery, Ala.: New South Books, 2011), 141–150.

Misconception 24

1. Email from LaVone Kay, marketing director, CAF Red Tail Squadron, with the Rise Above Traveling Exhibit, to Daniel Haulman in response to a question from Adolphus H. Bledsoe Jr.

2. Charlene Smith, *Tuskegee Airman: The Biography of Charles E. McGee, Air Force Fighter Combat Record Holder* (Boston: Branden Publishing Company, 1999), 174.

3. Telephone call from Alan Gropman to Daniel Haulman, July 29, 2013.

4. Billy J. Singleton, *Montgomery Aviation* (Charleston, S.C.: Arcadia Publishing, 2007), 126.

5. "The Volunteer States Goes to War: A Salute to Tennessee Veterans," electronic pamphlet issued by the Tennessee State Library and Archives.

6. Alabama Veterans Hall of Fame Society, Public Information, 2013; "Jim Cronk Flew 480 Combat Missions in Vietnam," War History Online, https://www.warhistoryonline.com/war-articles/jim-cronk-flew-480-combat-missions-vietnam.

7. Email from Jim Kilgus to Daniel Haulman, July 20, 2018. The number of fighter combat missions of Don Kilgus has not been confirmed in other documents.

8. John L. Frisbee, "The Pinnacle of Professionalism," *Air Force Magazine*, February 1987, 109; "Ralph S. Parr, Fighter Pilot," *Daedalus Flyer* 36, no. 2 (Summer 1996): 15–21; email from Barrett Tillman to Daniel Haulman, July 22, 2013.

9. John Mollison, *666, the Devil's Number: The Amazing Service of Hank Snow*, 2013, JohnMollison.com.

Misconception 25

1. Dr. John W. Kitchens, "They Also Flew: Pioneer Black Army Aviators," published in two consecutive issues of *U.S. Army Aviation Digest*, September/October and November/December 1994.

Misconception 26

1. James R. McGovern, Black Eagle: General Daniel 'Chappie' James, Jr. (Tuscaloosa: University of Alabama Press, 1985), 45–46.

2. Le Roy F. Gillead, The Tuskegee Aviation Experiment and Tuskegee Airmen, 1939–1949 (self-published, 1994); Emails from Alan Gropman to Daniel Haulman, July 29, 2013, and December 3, 2013; Emails from Guy Franklin to Daniel Haulman, December 3, 2013; Maj. John D. Murphy, "The Freeman Field Mutiny: A Study in Leadership," research paper written for Air Command and Staff College of Air University in March 1997.

3. James C. Warren, The Tuskegee Airmen Mutiny at Freeman Field (Vacaville, Calif.: Conyers Publishing Company, 1995), 34.

Misconception 27

1. Gail Buckley, American Patriots: The Story of Blacks in the Military from the Revolution to Desert Storm (New York: Random House, 2001), 277, 294.

2. Histories of the 99th Fighter Squadron at the Air Force Historical Research Agency (AFHRA).

3. Histories of the 332d Fighter Group and daily narrative mission reports of the group from January 1944 through April 1945 at the AFHRA.

4. 31st Fighter Group history for April 1945 at the AFHRA.

5. Lineage and honors histories of the 31st and 332d Fighter Groups.

6. Histories of the 57th Fighter Group and the 64th and 66th Fighter Squadrons.

7. Remarks by Arizona governor Jan Brewer on Arizona Senate Bill 1128, September 26, 2013.

8. 57th Fighter Group history.

9. Maurer Maurer, Air Force Combat Units of World War II (Washington, D.C.: Office of Air Force History, 1983), 120, 212.

Misconception 28

1. LeRoy Gillead, The Tuskegee Aviation Experiment and Tuskegee Airmen, 1939–1949 (San Francisco, Calif.: Balm-Bomb in Gillead, 1994), 67, 69, 71.

2. Gillead, Tuskegee Aviation Experiment, 71.

3. Narrative mission reports of the 332d Fighter Group between early June 1944 and the end of April 1945, contained in monthly histories of the group prepared by the 332d Fighter Group during the war.

Misconception 29

1. Victoria Wolk, "Member of Tuskegee Airmen Visits North Penn School District for Black History Month," Montgomery News, February 25, 2014; John Holway, Red Tails: An Oral History of the Tuskegee Airmen (Mineola, N.Y.: Dover Publications,

2011), 11; Lawrence P. Scott and William M. Womack Jr., Double V: The Civil Rights Struggle of the Tuskegee Airmen (East Lansing: Michigan State University Press, 1992), 41; Robert J. Jakeman, The Divided Skies (Tuscaloosa: University of Alabama Press, 1992), 8.

2. Cheryl Allison, "Many Calling on U.S. Postal Service to Honor Bryn Mawr Native, Tuskegee Airman C. Alfred 'Chief' Anderson in Stamp," Mainline Media News, February 3, 2014, http://www.mainlinemedianews.com; Pope Brock, "Chief Anderson," People Magazine, November 28, 1998; C. Alfred Anderson Legacy Foundation, "Father of Black Aviation," http://chief anderson.com.

3. J. Todd Moye, Freedom Flyers: The Tuskegee Airmen of World War II (Oxford, UK: Oxford University Press, 2010), 45; Von Hardesty, Black Wings: Courageous Stories of African Americans in Aviation and Space History (New York: HarperCollins, 2008), 52; Samuel L. Broadnax, Blue Skies, Black Wings: African American Pioneers of Aviation (Lincoln: University of Nebraska Press, 2007), 19; Allison, "Many Calling."

4. Tuskegee Army Air Field history, March–April 1945, vol. 1, Air Force Historical Research Agency(AFHRA), call number 289.28-9.

Misconception 30

1. Charlene E. McGee Smith, Tuskegee Airman: The Biography of Charles E. McGee (Boston: Branden Publishing Company, 1999), 28.

2. Robert J. Jakeman, The Divided Skies (Tuscaloosa: University of Alabama Press, 1992), 98, 102–103.

3. Jakeman, Divided Skies, 183.

4. LeRoy Gillead, The Tuskegee Aviation Experiment and Tuskegee Airmen, 1939–1949 (San Francisco, Calif.: Balm-Bomb in Gillead, 1994), 22–23.

5. Jakeman, Divided Skies, 187, 197, 206, 211, 221, 228, 240; War Department Adjutant General letter 320.2 February 18, 1941, (effective March 19, 1941)

6. Charles W. Dryden, A Train: Memoirs of a Tuskegee Airman (Tuscaloosa: University of Alabama Press, 1997), 110–111; J. Todd Moye, Freedom Flyers (Oxford, UK: Oxford University Press, 2010), 37–38.

Misconception 31

1. Lt. Col. Michael Lee Lanning, The African-American Soldier (New York: Citadel Press, 2004), 191.

2. J. Todd Moye, Freedom Flyers (Oxford, UK: Oxford University Press, 2010), 31–32; Robert J. Jakeman, The Divided Skies (Tuscaloosa: University of Alabama Press, 1992), 188–189, 201–202.

Misconception 32

1. Wikipedia article on C. Alfred "Chief" Anderson, accessed on March 18, 2014; newspaper articles published in March 2014 regarding the announcement of a new U.S. Postal Service stamp often made it appear that Charles "Chief" Anderson was the most important of all the flight instructors at Tuskegee when, in reality, he was involved in only the first of the three flight-training phases.

2. Histories of Tuskegee Army Air Field, Air Force Historical Research Agency(AFHRA), call numbers 289.28-9 and 289.28-10.

Misconception 33

1. Aaron J. McKean, America's Beautiful National Parks (Atlanta, Ga.: Whitman Publishing, 2014), 120.
2. Histories of Tuskegee Army Air Field, 2143d Army Air Forces Base Unit, 1941–1946, Air Force Historical Research Agency(AFHRA), call number 289.28.
3. Robert J. Jakeman, *The Divided Skies* (Tuscaloosa: University of Alabama Press, 1992), 245.

Misconception 34

1. Score sheets from the 1949 USAF gunnery meet at Las Vegas, Nev., voucher no. 40, furnished by 99 ABW historian Gerald A. White Jr.

Misconception 35

1. USAF Historical Study 81, USAF Credits for the Destruction of Enemy Aircraft, Korean War (Washington, D.C.: Office of Air Force History, 1975; Aces and Aerial Victories: The United States Air force in Southeast Asia, 1965–1973 (Washington, D.C.: Office of Air Force History, 1976).
2. Howard C. "Scrappy" Johnson, Scrappy: Memoir of a U.S. Fighter Pilot in Korea and Vietnam (Ian A. O. C. McFarland, 2007), 119.

Misconception 36

1. Benjamin O. Davis Jr., *Benjamin O. Davis, Jr., American* (Washington, D.C.: Smithsonian Institution Press, 1991), 48; National Aviation Hall of Fame Website, under Benjamin O. Davis Jr.
2. Alexander M. Bielakowski, "Benjamin O. Davis, Jr.," in *Ethnic and Racial Minorities in the U.S. Military: An Encyclopedia*, vol. 1, ed. Alexander M. Bielakowski (Santa Barbara, Calif.: (ABC-CLIO, 2013), 148.

Misconception 37

1. The author attended some ceremonies in Tuskegee in which he heard Col. Roosevelt Lewis called a "second-generation Tuskegee Airman."

Misconception 38

1. Public Law 109-213, 109th Congress, April 11, 2006, section 2.
2. The author watched the Tuskegee Airmen Gold Medal ceremony that was broadcast on national television on March 29, 2007. He also saw the original Gold Medal on display at the National Air and Space Museum in Washington, D.C., in 2014, and ordered a replica of the medal, which he donated to the National World War II Museum.
3. One example is John McCaskill, who attempted to honor a Tuskegee Airman who had missed the Gold Medal ceremony in Washington, D.C., in March 2007, and who he thought deserved to receive a Congressional Gold Medal too.

4. S. Sgt. Richard Wrigley, "95-Year-Old Tuskegee Air(wo)man Receives Congressional Gold Medal," Army News Service, April 21, 2015.

5. Charles M. Murphy, "Tuskegee Airman, Lt. Col. Leo Gray, Speaks at Okeechobee Correctional," Okeechobee News, April 23, 2015.

6. The author saw a sign with the Tuskegee Airmen Congressional Gold Medal at the National Air and Space Museum, which noted that it was now the property of the National Museum of African American History and Culture.

7. S. H. Kelly, "Seven World War II Veterans to Receive Medals of Honor," Army News Service, 1997.

Misconception 39

1. Telephone conversation between Lt. Col. Leo Gray and Daniel Haulman, March 30, 2015.

Misconception 40

1. "Dr. Russell Minton, 87, Talks about the Real History of the Tuskegee Airmen," You-Tube video of Dr. Russell Minton, recorded in January 2015, https://www.youtube .com/watch?v=16-4veOJFC4, and a May 20, 2015, email from Ron Albers to Daniel Haulman, referring to a meeting at Osceola High School in Kissimmee, Florida, in the spring of 2015.

2. Histories of the 99th Fighter Squadron at the Air Force Historical Research Agency; Robert Goralski, World War II Almanac, 1931–1945 (New York: G. P. Putnam's Sons, 1981), 260, 265–266.

Misconception 41

1. Ted Johnson database maintained by the Harry A. Sheppard Research Committee of the Tuskegee Airmen Incorporated.

2. Army Air Forces Statistical Digest, 1946, covering the years of World War II, 23, table 16; Lawrence J. Paszek, "Negroes and the Air Force, 1939–1949," Air University manuscript on file at the Air Force Historical Research Agency.

3. Alan L. Gropman, The Air Force Integrates, 1945–1964 (Washington, D.C.: Office of Air Force History, 1985), 8.

Misconception 42

1. Jeff Jardine, "Tuskegee Airmen Pilot, 91, Wants Record Set Straight," Modesto Bee, August 26, 2015.

2. Robert Goralski, World War II Almanac, 1931–1945 (New York: G. P. Putnam's Sons, 1981), 404.

3. 306 Fighter Wing Composite Mission Reports for May 1945. The May 7, 1945, report is numbered 176. These documents are stored at the Air Force Historical Research Agency (AFHRA) under call number WG-306-HI, May 1945. The IRIS reference number is 00109052. The 332d Fighter Group history for May 1945 is consistent. Its call number is GP-332-HI, May 1945.

4. 306 Fighter Wing Composite Mission Report number 176, as of 2000 hours, May 7, 1945.

5. Lineage and honors history of the 332d Fighter Group (later 332d Air Expeditionary Group); May 1945 history of the 332d Fighter Group; Maurer Maurer, Combat Squadrons of the Air Force, World War II (Washington, D.C.: U.S. Government Printing Office, 1969), 329, 332, 365.

6. 332d Fighter Group history, May 1945, at the AFHRA.

7. Kit C. Carter and Robert Mueller, editors, The Army Air Forces in World War II Combat Chronology, 1941–1945 (N.p.: Albert F. Simpson Historical Research Center and Office of Air Force History, 1973), 647.

8. Fifteenth Air Force Mission Reports for May 1945, AFHRA, call number 670.332 and the date.

Misconception 43

1. An example is the account of the incident in Gail Buckley's American Patriots: The Story of Blacks in the Military from the Revolution to Desert Storm (New York: Random House, 2001).

2. Lt. Col. James C. Warren, The Tuskegee Airmen Mutiny at Freeman Field (Vacaville, Calif.: Conyers Publishing Company, 1995). Warren was one of those arrested, and he lists the others who were arrested with him.

Misconception 44

1. Experience of author at an art exhibit at Troy University Montgomery, where a Tuskegee Airmen exhibit was presented. For the locations of the Tuskegee Airmen combat units during World War II, see the histories of the 99th, 100th, 301st, and 302d Fighter Squadrons and of the 332d Fighter Group during the period 1943–1945.

2. Lineage and honors histories of the Eighth, Ninth, and Fifteenth Air Forces; June history of the 332d Fighter Group and of the 99th Fighter Squadron. These histories are available at the Air Force Historical Research Agency.

3. Histories of the 477th Bombardment Group (later, 477th Composite Group) during World War II.

Misconception 45

1. Maj. Welton I. Taylor and Karyn J. Taylor, Two Steps from Glory: A World War II Liaison Pilot Confronts Jim Crow and the Enemy in the South Pacific (Chicago: Winning Strategy Press, 2012), 89, 208; list of Tuskegee Airmen liaison pilots in David G. Styles, The Tuskegee Airmen and Beyond: The Road to Equality (Deerfield, Ill.: Dalton Watson Fine Books), 259.

Misconception 46

1. Plate on trophy for the 1949 winners of the Las Vegas gunnery meet, which lists the 4th Fighter Group as having won first place in the jet class, and the 332d Fighter Group as having won first place in the conventional class.

2. Richard P. Hallion, Storm over Iraq (Washington, D.C.: Smithsonian Institution Press, 1992), 31.

Misconception 47

1. Centers for Disease Control and Prevention Tuskegee Timeline, https://www.cdc.gov /tuskegee/timeline.htm.
2. Mary Meehan, "Memory Sunday: Churches Spread Alzheimer's Awareness," http:// ohiovalleyrecourse.org/2017/08/01memory-sunday-churches-spread-alzheimers -awareness.
3. The incident occurred when I was presenting a lecture about the Tuskegee Airmen at the main branch of the Mobile Public Library on June 30, 2011. There were about seventy-five people in the audience, but I did not record the name of the person who made the assertion.

Misconception 48

1. Charles E. Francis, *Tuskegee Airmen: The Men Who Changed a Nation* (Wellesley, Mass.: Branden Books, 2008). This edition of the book, edited by Adolph Caso, was the fifth edition of the first, which was published by the Bruce Humphrey Company.

Misconception 49

1. Telephone conversation between Mary Doll of the National Park Service and Daniel Haulman of the Air Force Historical Research Agency (AFHRA), March 5, 2018.
2. Lineage and honors histories of the listed organizations and their organizational re- cord cards, AFHRA,, Research Division, Organizational Histories section, Maxwell Air Force Base, Ala.

Misconception 50

1. Daily narrative mission reports of the 332d Fighter Group for July 1944, Air Force Historical Research Agency (AFHRA), call number GP-332-HI (FTR), July 1944.

Misconception 51

1. Phillip Thomas Tucker, *Father of the Tuskegee Airmen, John C. Robinson* (Washington, D.C.: Potomac Books, 2012), 67, 71, 78; Gail Buckley, *American Patriots: The Story of Blacks in the Military from the Revolution to Desert Storm* (New York: Random House, 2001), 251–253; Abraham Lincoln Brigade Archives, www.alba-valb.org/volunteers /browse/james-lincoln-holt-peck.

Misconception 52

1. Biographies files of USAF leaders at the Air Force Historical Research Agency (AFHRA).
2. Gen. Daniel James Jr. personal papers at the AFHRA, including Air Force Form 17, created on July 1948 and completed by him on November 25, 1949, which states clearly that while Gen. James attended Tuskegee Institute between 1937 and 1941, he received no degree. Air Force Form 11, January 1966 edition, which James completed on March 26, 1970, notes clearly that he received his bachelor of science degree in physical education in 1969. J. Alfred Phelps, *Chappie: America's First Black Four-Star General, the Life and Times of Daniel James, Jr.* (Novato, Calif.: Presidio Press, 1991), 16, 21, 265–266; James R. McGovern, *Black Eagle: General Daniel 'Chappie' James, Jr.* (Tuscaloosa: University of Alabama Press, 1985), 30, 119.

Misconception 53

1. Author's experience at eight Tuskegee Airmen National Conventions (in 2007, 2008, 2009, 2010, 2011, 2012, 2014, and 2015) and conversations with the heads of the Harry Sheppard Research Team/Committee: Robert Holloman, George Hardy, and James Crump.

Misconception 54

1. Historical Studies Branch, USAF Historical Division, *Combat Crew Rotation: World War II and Korean War* (Maxwell AFB, Ala.: Aerospace Studies Institute, Air University, 1968), 12–14; Dennis Hevesi, "Colonel Donald Blakeslee, Decorated World War II Ace, Dies at 90," *New York Times*, October 3, 2008; John Mollison, *666, the Devil's Number: The Amazing Service of Hank Snow*, 2013, JohnMollison.com.

Misconception 55

1. Stephen L. McFarland and Wesley Phillips Newton, *To Command the Sky: The Battle for Air Superiority over Germany, 1942–1944* (Washington, D.C.: Smithsonian Institution Press, 1991), 190.

2. 332d Fighter Group daily narrative mission reports, filed with the histories of the group by month, June 1944 through April 1945, at the Air Force Historical Research Agency, Maxwell Air Force Base, Ala.

3. Williamson Murray and Allan R. Millett, *A War to Be Won* (Cambridge, Mass.: Belknap Press of Harvard University Press, 2000), 325.

Index